FINDING REAL
PURPOSE

Kenneth
NKEMNACHO

© 2012 Kenneth Nkemnacho
info@ kennethvisionmedia.com

Published by www.kennethvisionmedia.com
Second Edition

ISBN: 978-0-9568373-9-4

DEDICATION

This book is dedicated to:

My committed wife:
Ruth Abosede Nkemnacho
My joy-bringing children: Godfavour and Joshua.

TABLE OF CONTENTS

ACKNOWLEDGEMENT.. 7

THE MEANING OF PURPOSE... 9

CHARACTERISTICS OF DIVINE PURPOSE...............…………...... 21

THE ORIGINAL PURPOSE……………..........…….…........................ 31

THE RENEWED PURPOSE...............……….........…….………............. 81

HOW TO DISCOVER YOUR PURPOSE…......…….……….................. 91

WALKING IN DIVINE PURPOSE...............….……………............ 105

THE SIGNIFICANCE AND BENEFITS OF DIVINE PURPOSE..... 119

INHIBITORS OF DIVINE PURPOSE......…….……………….. 135

DIMENSIONAL PURPOSE....................…….………………….. 153

CONCLUSION...............................…….…………….. 177

ABOUT THE AUTHOR.. 179

ACKNOWLEDGMENT

To God, who gives the knowledge, understanding, wisdom, power, strength, and protection be glory forever and ever. Amen. When you set out to do something in line with divine purpose, the forces of hell will rage violently against you just like the maddening storm that hit the boat of Jesus Christ. In this seemingly unending situation, you will keep hearing the voice of God saying, 'Be still and know that I am God'. In the course of writing this book, the forces of hell waged a fierce battle against me and my family. There were occasions when I literarily wept, but God continued to be my comfort. He never left me; neither did He forsake me nor my family. He proved to me that the God of purpose is the God of provision. For this, I am very grateful.

To my wife, who is able to endure the dream of a Christian writer coupled with her commitment to God, family, and work, I deep-heartedly appreciate you. You've been an inspiration, especially when you get up in the night to tap me on the shoulders as I sit on the computer. These are not mere touches, they carry power.

We started the writing of this book on a traditional pen and paper method. I guess we were just being old fashioned but my beloved sister, Ifeoma Ezelue, embarked on the typing of the manuscript. It's an unusual sacrifice for a woman with four little angels to commit day and night typing one boy's manuscript. Thank you mama!

To all who took the time to read the manuscript and made very important contributions, God bless you. May you receive abundance of grace in Jesus' name. Amen.

To Pastor Matthew Ashimolowo and Pastor Dipo Oluyomi, how can I express my thanks for the precious time you took out of your busy schedules to read my manuscript and gave such productive feedbacks? May God reward you beyond your prayers and hopes in Jesus' name. Amen.

To Xllingua, you are the best in what you do. Who can fault this? Keep being fantastic. You did put a spark into this book.

You can't stop appreciating Kingsway International Christian Centre (KICC); a great church with the great God and great leadership. It's a church built on divine purpose and due diligence.

God bless you.

Kenneth Nkemnacho

THE MEANING OF PURPOSE

Imagine yourself being offered a job in a certain organisation. On your appointment letter, your job description is spelled out. This job description becomes your guide to the roles and responsibilities assigned to you by the company. Your performance will be assessed and evaluated according to these stipulated responsibilities.

Man was created with a job description. Each person was made with a specific responsibility to perform on earth. An identification of this duty gives man the direction to the pathway to walk on earth. This pathway is the destiny of man. This destiny is the real purpose for creation.

Ephesians 1:11-12 (New King James Version)
'In Him also we have obtained an inheritance, being predestined according to the purpose of Him who works all things according to the counsel of His will, that we who first trusted in Christ should be to the praise of His glory.'

It is expedient for man to understand that the key to divine purpose is inheritance. Some people question the existence of destiny without realising that if there is a Creator, there must be an intention. Real purpose is not defined by man but by God. Purpose is not a suggestion; it is a motive borne out of heritage. It is passed on to humanity by Divinity.

When a man walks out of purpose, he struggles. Billions of people on earth are attempting to define their own destinies. In doing so, they completely miss the track. In life, there is a track. The track is that divine assignment that prompts a man's creativity. What we all need to know is that we cannot create destinies for ourselves when they are already created. What man therefore needs to do is search for his reason for existence, instead of making a counterfeit.

1Corinthians 3:11 (New King James Version)
'For no other foundation can anyone lay than that which is laid, which is Jesus Christ.'

If God has laid a foundation, the willingness of man to build on it makes his walk of destiny established. Destroying a divine foundation in order to lay another foundation is counter-productive to God's purpose in the person's life. When God creates, He predestines. Walking in original destiny is walking in real purpose. Those who walk in real purpose are divinely guided. When you follow this guide, you end up at the right destination. Where you end up becomes your final home. Some people have ended in divine fulfilment, peace, joy, and heaven. Others, who chose to go their own way, have also reaped the consequences of straying away. Your destination is your choice, and your choice is a decision. Some decisions derail and defeat divine intention, while other decisions, guided by biblical principles, produce eternal rewards. You cannot find real purpose and become purposeless. No one who walks in divine purpose becomes defeated in life, no matter how turbulent things may be. To get the best in life, search to know who you are, and why you were created. Your blessing is tied to your divine purpose on earth. When you find this heritage that was designed for you, walk in it.

Isaiah 30:21 (New King James Version)
'Your ears shall hear a word behind you, saying, " This is the way,
walk in it," whenever you turn to the right hand or whenever you
turn to the left.'

Your ability to hear what is behind you is a key to knowing your destination. Your hearing skill cannot be separated from your destiny. Some people are deaf to what is behind them. Others hear it and ignore it. A few hear, follow, and obtain the right result.

The type and number of words you hear behind you determine who the speaker is, and what he's saying. Divine purpose is not a talkative. The Bible says, 'Your ears shall hear a word behind you' not words. A decision taking a man nowhere is always equivocal. Ignorance talks too much. Any ambition carried out without God's approval is a noise maker.

Divine purpose does not encourage partial deafness. You must be willing to hear with both ears. It is both ears that should hear a word behind you, not one of them. Divine purpose does not suffer from illusion. You can't give one ear to God and the other to yourself or side attractions. Your ear cannot incline to purpose and your actions not fit for purpose.

Real purpose always has the way, not a way. Its route and direction are well defined. You can't miss its path if you're willing to follow. Divine purpose will push you back on track when you stray left or right. In following your destiny, you will realise that your right may not be God's right.

WHAT IS PURPOSE?

Sometime ago, someone I know made a life changing statement that touched my heart. He said, 'My pain is that I don't

11

know who I am. I'm still trying to find out who I am.' What hit me most about the speaker was that he was already in his forties. Then, it occurred to me that most people have lived and died without fulfilling their mandates on earth. I am of a very strong opinion that it is better to discover a destiny late and walk in it, as opposed to not realising it at all. It is a disaster to deviate from the course of destiny. A lot of people have either derailed from purpose or were never in it. If you go to the street to ask people what their purposes in life are, you will be shocked to realise that many people don't know what it's all about.

Purpose is defined as:

- A fixed design, outcome, or idea that is the object of an action.
- The reason for which anything is done, created, or exists.
- Fixed intention in doing something, and the determination to achieve it.

Where there is purpose there is determination, aspiration, expectation, proposition, and confidence.

Psalm 90:12 (New King James Version)
'So teach us to number our days, that we may gain a heart of wisdom.'

Divine purpose is wisdom. The mathematics of reality is key to purpose discovery. God Himself is the Teacher, who gives the equation or formula that produces the right answer.

If a man can number his days, he should be able to apply his heart to wisdom. But the unfortunate thing is that some people number their days but still end up doing foolish things. It is your responsibility to apply wisdom after you have been taught. Being taught is being armed with information. A waste of information is a wasted purpose. The ability to number one's days is a second chance given by God for a person to step back into divine purpose. Instead of stepping back, some people use that time to mourn over what has been lost rather than doing something. They always feel that it is too late. Divine purpose is never too late. How can something that is inheritable be too late? If you don't complete it, pass it on.

Ecclesiastes 3:1 (New King James Version)
'To everything there is a season, a time for every purpose under heaven.'

There is timing in divine purpose; you cannot rush it. Wandering into anything without understanding its purpose is sheer foolishness. Winning in life requires purpose. A purposeless person is an aimless person. If everything has a purpose, you must not support in life a decision that has no foundation. People may consider you too strict; just keep your focus.

THE FOUNDATIONS OF PURPOSE

There are certain blocks that form the foundation of purpose. Without them, purpose cannot be established. These are:

Aim: aim is positioning, direction, target, focus, and precision. It is the direction in which something is pointed with the optimum reason of obtaining a desired result. Purpose without aim is misdirection. Hunters know the importance of aiming before shooting. If you shoot without aim, you may end up killing an innocent person. Firing a purpose without aim makes purpose a stray bullet.

1 Samuel 17:49 (New King James Version)
'Then David put his hand in his bag and took out a stone; and he slung it and struck the Philistine in his forehead, so that the stone sank into his forehead, and he fell on his face to the earth.'

13

The first principle in aim is that you must have an appropriate weapon. You can't hit a target with the wrong weapon. If a target requires a stone, you must not use a spear. It is not the material content of a weapon that gives victory but the One behind it. You may have the best education, yet miss your target in life. You may even be in the best profession, but yet remain unsatisfied. Until you aim for your call, your soul will keep yearning for something you cannot figure out.

The second principle is that you must have no phobia for target attainment. Targets are always intimidating at first sight, but when you approach them with boldness, they submit to you. Goliaths always brag but end up falling face down, and with their own weapons, their heads are cut off. Your stone may be small, but when your positive character is big, the enemies will be put to flight. Never allow the size of challenges intimidate your destiny. Don't look at your capacity to determine your ability to reach the desire of God for your life. Divine purpose is not your own making, neither are you responsible for fulfilling it. Your responsibility is to discover it, walk in it, and God will fulfil it.

The principle of running towards your target is a step of faith. Targets never move towards you until you run towards them. Goliaths don't move until you move. If you attempt to hit your destiny from a long distance, you will misfire. If you can't go close you can't meet purpose. Those who avoid the battle of destiny never get fulfilled. The fight they run from ends up killing them prematurely.

When you aim, take a shot. Some people have come close to destiny without taking a shot. If you don't shoot you can't conquer. Don't let the fear of failure prevent you from firing the bullet of divine purpose. No one who follows real purpose fails. Victory is sure for those who challenge the giants who defy progress.

Intention: intention is the reason behind purpose. It is the end, object, act, and fact of purpose. The reason behind purpose is the motive behind destiny. Motive gives you the drive towards an expected result.

Colossians 3:2 (New King James Version)
'Set your mind on things above, not on things on the earth.'

Divine purpose is heavenly-minded. Your purpose is above when your mind is set to please God and not yourself. A mind that pleases God is not manipulated by the side attractions of earthly gains. If you have a purpose that is earth bound, that purpose may be your personal agenda. Where your mind is set is where your tomorrow lies. If your intention does not agree with an upward setting of mind, your goal is not heavenly. For you to go far above mediocrity, your target must be far beyond the ordinary. You can live on earth and operate in the heavens, if you understand how and where to position your mind.

Matthew 6:21 (New king James Version)
'For where your treasure is, there your heart will be also.'

Your treasure should be your divine intention not your personal agenda. Treasure can be geographically located. The easiest way to judge a man's value system is to look at where his attention is. His heart is where his attention is. You can't separate a man's heart from the location of his treasure. In modern day geography, remote sensing is used in studying remote geographical areas that are impossible for man to reach. This technology uses high tech cameras to obtain still and moving images which give ideas of what those areas look like. To understand divine purpose, there must be mental remote sensing. In this sensing, there must be an analysis of intention and reason for desiring to walk in divine purpose. If we can picture the remote areas of our lives, we can easily correct wrong intentions for wanting to live in our callings. If a man's heart is in divine purpose, he will find divine treasure.

Therefore, let your heart be on God's intention for your life, so that you can be heavenly retained. Retention comes from being chosen. There are lots of people who are called into divine purpose, but lose out to wrong motives. Wrong motives lead to rejection. Many are called, few are retained.

Goal: is the result or achievement towards which effort is directed. It is the terminal point in a race or journey, or the area where points are scored.

People talk about setting goals, but I believe more in scoring goals. I respect the fact that it takes skills to set up goals, howbeit, we should realise that some people have set up goals but couldn't score, and ended up losing the game. Life is more than a game, far more serious than a game, and the one who scores is the one who wins. A purpose without goal scoring is a fruitless purpose.

Mark 9:49-50 (New King James Version)
'For everyone will be seasoned with fire, and every sacrifice will be seasoned with salt. Salt is good, but if the salt loses its flavor, how will you season it? Have salt in yourselves, and have peace with one another.'

A purpose without divine goal is like salt without flavour. The objective of salt is to season, preserve, and flavour. If it cannot achieve any of these functions, it becomes useless. If there is no divine goal, purpose becomes tasteless and unpreserved. This is why so many people, after achieving so much in life, remain despondent and dissatisfied. Some end up committing suicide.

If you don't fulfil divine mandate, you will leave a divine vacuum in that corner of your heart that no material wealth can fill. Divine purpose takes you through a seasoning with fire. When you get roasted or grilled, you become a treasure that can withstand time and spoilage. To increase your longevity, salt will be added to you. This salt will season, preserve, and add flavour to your life. If your purpose has not gone through fire, you need to do some soul search. Jesus said, 'For EVERYONE will be seasoned with fire, and EVERY sacrifice will be seasoned with salt'. When God says everyone, He means everyone. If you take yourself out of the equation of EVERYONE, your agenda becomes personal.

Design: every purpose must have a blueprint. A design is the preparation of a preliminary sketch or plan for a work to be executed. It is artistically and skilfully done. It is a drawing, structure, or decorative scheme that can be assigned a thought, formed or conceived in the mind.

A purpose with a design is a purpose with a destination. The design of a purpose is the picture painted or printed on paper or the mind. It is the plan written in black and white, or constructively imagined on the screens of the mind. A design is a motivator and an inspiration that drives you towards achieving your set goals. Beholding the design gives you an idea of how much effort you're making towards fulfilling your divine mandate.

Genesis 6:15-16 (New King James Version)
'And this is how you shall make it: The length of the ark shall be three hundred cubits, its width fifty cubits, and its height thirty cubits. You shall make a window for the ark, and you shall finish it to a cubit from above; and set the door of the ark in its side. You shall make it with lower, second, and third decks.'

When God says, *'And this is how you shall make it'*, it means there is no other way to make it beyond following His design. God never gives a purpose without giving it a design. When He gives a purpose, He gives the specific measurements, whether in length, width, height, or breadth. His purpose has a window for illumination and freshness, and a door for exit and entry. He does not force anyone. Purpose is a choice.

In God's design of purpose, there are levels. There is the lower, second, and third deck. His design is promotional. You move from level to level, depending on your commitment. If you end up in the first level, it means you did not pass the test for higher levels. It takes a lot of sacrifice to be on the third deck.

2 Corinthians 12:2 (New King James Version)
'I know a man in Christ who fourteen years ago—whether in the body I do not know, or whether out of the body I do not know, God knows—such a one was caught up to the third heaven.'

To reach the third deck, you must be in Christ. It is not human effort that takes you there, but your submission to the One who is the Father of the third heaven. It is a level that makes you speechless. It is an environment where your personal knowledge becomes useless.

God's design of purpose is overwhelming. When you follow this design, you profit far beyond human imagination.

Proposition: this is a prototype of a design subjected to consideration, understudy, and scrutiny before adoption. Purpose must have a proposition. When you find divine destiny, make a prototype and study it. Let other people who have gone through that road successfully also be involved in scrutinising your proposition. Don't just run into things even if they're real. Count the cost and prepare to pay the price. If you have no proposition, you won't understand the amount of sacrifice required to achieve your destiny. If you lack understanding, you will get frustrated in the middle of the journey.

God is the God of proposition. His intention was to bring into being the new covenant, but He started by making a prototype.

The Old Testament is a prototype of the New. The New was God's purpose for humanity, but He first made the Old, and subjected it to scrutiny, consideration, and study.

Colossians 2:16-17 (New King James Version)
'So let no one judge you in food or in drink, or regarding a festival or a new moon or sabbaths, which are a shadow of things to come, but the substance is of Christ.'

The presence of a shadow means there is a substance nearby. The shadow may not be the real thing, but it gives you a clue and guide towards reaching the substance. When you study the shadow, you will get to the deep meanings of what it represents. As you study, you realise that *'there are things to come'*. As you behold the shadow, let your inner man picture the things to come. There is power in picturing unseen things. This power is the force behind a vision. When your inner eyes are seeing clearly, you cannot end up in shadows. Physical men end up in food, drink, festivals, astrology, and religion but spiritual men are judged by substance. Your substance in Christ should be your purpose in life. Life and purpose without Christ is a dream without substance.

Determination: determination is -

- The quality of being resolute, and firmness of purpose.
- Ascertainment after observation or investigation.
- The act or instance of making a decision.

Determination involves persistence, conviction, dedication, and resolution. A determined heart never looks back. It is consumed with the zeal of bringing divine purpose to reality. Determination does not tolerate time wastage. It is always target-oriented.

Nehemiah 4:6 (New King James Version)
'So we built the wall, and the entire wall was joined together up to half it's height, for the people had a mind to work.'

The sentence, 'For the people had a mind to work', is a statement of oneness and determination. Where there is determination there is unity! One heart, one mind, one thought, one focus, and one target is the key to achieving real purpose. A double minded person cannot get to the finish line of destiny. He cannot even hit any target. Double minded people fire stray bullets. Never align with a man who is not stable in decision making. He can start with you but leave you stranded in the middle of the road.

Determination brings purpose to completion. Against all odds, it finishes well. Determination is not a time waster. It works day and night to accomplish destiny. It is not lazy, does not make excuses, and never gets fed up when things are unfavourable.

If you apply a determined heart towards real purpose, you are bound to win. Excellence cannot be separated from the person who perseveres and fights to reach the end of a purposeful race. If you dare to achieve, you will finish with a smile!

CHARACTERISTICS
OF
DIVINE PURPOSE

Characteristics are distinguishing features or peculiar qualities that typify an objective, pursuit, or a thing. They are marks of distinctions and dispositions.

Real purpose has indications. These indications are the features that separate divine purpose from personal ambitions. Some of the characteristics that help you identify divine purpose are:

Divine purpose is God-given: strategies and good plans can fail, if they are not God-given. Sometimes, people can even be successful without God being in it. The difference between God-given success and personal success is that the first is good while the second may be ordinary or bad. Success in personal pursuit is earthly and perishable, but divine success is eternal and heavenly. No mot and rot can eat up God-given success, but the worms of economic crisis and other challenges evaporate the gains of earthly ambitions.

Matthew 6:11 (New King James Version)
'Give us this day our daily bread.'

God is responsible for giving *'this day'*. The day carries the destiny, and in the destiny is divine purpose. In divine purpose, you will find the bread for living. If you eat any other bread, you will die, but if you eat the one that was given by Deity, you will live forever. If your bread of purpose is different from the one that has been divinely given, you are completely off track.

John 6:35 (New King James Version)
'And Jesus said to them, "I am the bread of life. He who comes to Me shall never hunger, and he who believes in Me shall never thirst."'

The bread of life is the bread of divine purpose. Eating the bread that has already been provided means you will never go hungry or thirsty. This is where true satisfaction comes from. If you eat anything else, no matter how delicious it may be, you can't get real life satisfaction. The hunger and thirst of fulfilment can only be quenched by consuming your God-given destiny.

Divine purpose is God-fulfilled: it is only the One who gives the plan that knows how to fulfil the plan. You can't do God's plan your own way and in your own time. When you discover purpose, also yearn to discover the methodology for fulfilment.

Isaiah 37:32 (New King James Version)
'For out of Jerusalem shall go a remnant, and those who escape from Mount Zion. The zeal of the LORD of hosts will do this.'

Zeal is an eager desire, endeavour, enthusiastic diligence, intensity, and passion to fulfil a course. The zeal of God is a performer and an achiever. God never gives a dream that cannot be fulfilled. His zeal is Spirit-driven, and His passion unquantifiable. When you depend on His zeal, no destiny is too big to attain. If God gives you a vision, never have a sleepless night on how it will materialise, because the Giver is the Fulfiller.

Divine purpose is a written document: divine purpose must be written in the heart and mind, and on paper. God is a Writer. He does not plan without writing. Anyone who wants to walk with God must be ready to write. If you don't write down His information, He won't give you more. God showed an example of writing with the way He fashioned out the Bible. The Bible is God's written document and constitution to the world. You cannot step into divine purpose, if you're a lazy writer. God ascertains your level of seriousness by how much you write down the vision He gives to you. Men of vision and purpose know the significance of noting down divine information.

Revelation 1:19 (New King James Version)
'Write the things which you have seen, and the things which are, and the things which will take place after this.'

You must be ready to write down what you see, because the things that you see are the things that will take place. In divine purpose, God will show you a bit of the future. This is what makes His purpose visionary. If you can't document this information, you won't be able to make reference to it when the time comes. If you cannot refer to it, you cannot know when the fulfilment comes. Those who don't document ascribe a victory to chance or hard work. The more you write the more you receive.

Divine purpose is simple and easy to understand: God's purpose is never confusing, neither is it complex. It may be challenging, and sometimes tough, but it still gives joy.

1 Corinthians 14:33 (New King James Version)
'For God is not the author of confusion but of peace, as in all the churches of the saints.'

Simplicity does not confuse; it brings peace. When a thing is simple, it becomes straightforward. A document written in straightforward language can be easily understood. When God gives you a vision, He will bring it down to your level of understanding. Anyone can understand the statement of divine purpose because it is plain and unequivocal.

Habakkuk 2:2 (New King James Version)
'Then the LORD answered me and said: " Write the vision and make it plain on tablets, that he may run who reads it."'

If your purpose makes no one run, it is not plain. It is a divine instruction that a man's destiny must be written in simple language for anyone to be able to read it. When a vision is understood, it will attract runners. Runners will help you take your divine dream to its desired destination. A vision is so simple to the extent that some people scorn it. Sometimes, when you declare your vision in life, foolish people make jest of you. If your declaration brings mockery, it means the vision is plainly understood. If your vision is plainly understood, it's an indication that you are already on step one to fulfilling divine purpose.

The summary of divine purpose is usually not more than two to three sentences: when God calls you, He gives you a summary of your life assignment. This summary must be your vision statement. A good vision statement does not exceed three sentences. This statement is what must keep ringing in your heart wherever you go. If you're going off track, it is your vision statement that will push you back on track. It must always be the centre of your focus. Day and night, you must keep hearing it with your inner ear.

Abraham's divine assignment was to carry the Seed of promise, who is Jesus Christ. Noah and Joseph the dreamer were divinely assigned to preserve lives. John the Baptist came to prepare the way for the Messiah, while Apostle Paul was called to minister mainly to the gentiles.

To achieve the best in your calling, your divine purpose must be your only goal. Never allow the summary of your calling evaporate from your heart even for a second. Do not allow man give you an alternative suggestion. Your destiny may mean nothing to carnal men, but it is your destiny. You will be judged according to your calling, not man's opinion.

Divine purpose must be specific: one of the characteristics of enzymes is that they are specific. As a result, one molecule of enzyme can digest thousands of molecules of a food substance. Specificity is definite, precise, and particular.

The key to performance is specificity. Specificity is target-driven. You can't aim at two targets the same time.

Acts 9:15 (New King James Version)
'But the Lord said to him, "Go, for he is a chosen vessel of Mine to bear My name before Gentiles, kings, and the children of Israel."'

The specificity of Apostle Paul's divine purpose was, 'To bear God's name'. As a symbol of bearing God's name, God changed his name from Saul to Paul. Saul means, 'Prayed for or responded', but Paul means, 'Small or humble'. If you're not humble, you cannot bear God's name. To fulfil divine destiny, you must make your personal ambition small until it completely disappears. It takes the attitude of humility to achieve that. Humility will drive you into and onto the path of specificity.

In specificity, there is also prioritisation. There were three major locations where Paul was going to bear God's name. The first was before the gentiles, then in front of kings, and lastly, before the children of Israel. That meant that the gentiles were his number one assignment. In purpose, you can't take the risk of starting from the least. Starting from the least is starting from your comfort zone. Some people have missed out on major assignments by settling for the least. If you settle for the least, your assignment will not be fulfilled.

Divine purpose is predestined: predestination is to destine in advance, foreordain, or predetermine. It is a determination beforehand.

Romans 8:30 (New King James Version)
'Moreover whom He predestined, these He also called; whom He called, these He also justified; and whom He justified, these He also glorified.'

A calling or divine purpose is predestined. This calling attracts justification, which advances into glorification. If you insist on following an un-predestined purpose, you're not walking in your calling. If you don't walk in your calling, you're not justified, and if not justified, there is no way you can be glorified.

Isaiah 60:1-2 (New King James Version)
'Arise, shine; for your light has come! And the glory of the LORD is risen upon you. For behold, the darkness shall cover the earth, and deep darkness the people; but the LORD will arise over you, and His glory will be seen upon you.'

The glory of the Lord can only be risen on those who walk in divine destiny. The Lord arises on those who follow His plan for them. But for those who are driven by their earthly ambitions, when the darkness covers the earth, they and their achievements will be lost in the dark.

Divine purpose is measurable and dimensional: God is a God of measurement and dimensions. Whatever He does, He measures and gives figures. This makes him very accountable. Divine purpose comes with accountability.

1 Kings 6:2 (New King James version)
'Now the house which King Solomon built for the LORD, its length was sixty cubits, its width twenty, and its height thirty cubits.'

Solomon's calling was to build the house of the Lord. In a bid to fulfil that purpose, God gave Him the measurement and dimension of the temple, and he stuck to that plan. He did not adjust it to suit his own purpose.

When God gives a purpose, He also gives the measurement and dimension. If you stick to the original plan, that is when you please Him, but if you adjust the specification a little bit, the variance in real life may be unbelievable.

James 3:4 (New King James Version)
'Look also at ships: although they are so large and are driven by fierce winds, they are turned by a very small rudder wherever the pilot desires.'

Using a personal desire rudder to adjust divine destiny may expose an individual to a fierce and boisterous wind. It is strongly advisable to follow the main plan, in order to feature in the main event.

Divine purpose has a time phase: there is a time phase for the beginning and end of a purpose. When God gives you a vision and says 'wait', you must wait. When He says, 'stop', you also need to stop. You can't go on with a plan when you haven't been divinely prompted, and you can't stop, when there is no Spiritual red signal. If you step in before time, you will be frustrated, and if you step out before maturation, your baby will be premature.

Ecclesiastes 3:1 (New King James Version)
'To everything there is a season, a time for every purpose under heaven.'

You can't adjust the timing for divine purpose. It is the Giver who is the Timer. When God says, 'It is time', you can't say, 'Let me go bury my dead father'. A divine call is a military order. You must leave everything behind and answer the call of duty.

Galatians 4:4-5 (New King James Version)
'But when the fullness of the time had come, God sent forth His Son, born of a woman, born under the law, to redeem those who were under the law, that we might receive the adoption as sons.'

There is a fullness of time for divine purpose. You can't hurry it; neither can you leave it a little longer.

Divine purpose comes with divine provision: divine provision always locates divine purpose without struggling. When God gives a vision, he makes a way for the vision.

Luke 8:3 (New King James Version)
'And Joanna the wife of Chuza, Herod's steward, and Susanna, and many others who provided for Him from their substance.'

Chuza was a top official in the government of Herod Antipas. It is unimaginable to think that part of the resources that funded the ministry of Jesus Christ came from an enemy camp. When you follow God's plan, wonders will never cease to happen. The money, materials and people needed to bring your dream to reality will be divinely positioned in your way.

Divine purpose appears foolish at inception: when Noah started building the ark, he was ridiculed. The foolishness of building a gigantic ship on dry land with no sea is laughable. People may laugh at your vision, and tell you how impossible it is to achieve, but the onus is on you to believe in what you have been called to do, and to stick to it. You must approach your destiny with the attitude of faith, independent of what unbelievers think or say about it. The unbelievers may be your spouse, friends, Pastors, or colleagues. Once you're convinced that God is behind your endeavours, fight the good fight of faith. Destiny actualisation is a fight of purpose.

Hebrews 11:7 (New King James Version)
'By faith Noah, being divinely warned of things not yet seen, moved

with godly fear, prepared an ark for the saving of his household, by which he condemned the world and became an heir of the righteousness which is according to faith.'

Sticking to divine purpose is standing on the ground of faith. You can hear God clearly when you're in His will. Being in His will produce godly fear, and this fear drives you to carry out His instructions. When you carry out His instructions, you will become an heir of righteousness by faith.

Divine purpose floats on despair: a purpose that is from God cannot sink in the flood.

A vision that is divine cannot collapse. The storms and flood will beat it hard, but it will stand. When the flood of despair sweeps ambitions away, divine visions will float on the troubled waters.

Genesis 7:8 (New King James Version)
'The waters prevailed and greatly increased on the earth, and the ark moved about on the surface of the waters.'

If your purpose is earthly, the waters of destruction will prevail and greatly converge on it when the flood comes. But if it is heavenly, when the flood comes against it, your ark can only move towards where it belongs; up. Going up is the only option in the flood for those with divine purpose. If your treasure is in the heavens, when trouble comes, you will move towards where your treasure is, but if on earth, you will remain down.

Divine purpose makes a sacrificial offering that defies scarcity: heavenly purpose appreciates protection, and offers sacrifices that defy scarcity.

Genesis 8:20 (New King James Version)
'Then Noah built an altar to the LORD, and took of every clean animal and of every clean bird, and offered burnt offerings on the altar.'

The number of animals in the ark was very limited; yet, Noah offered sacrifices from that scarcity. He took the best from his limited resources and gave to God. He put God first before his family, and animal rights. He risked the extinction of certain species of animals. This was why it was ascribed to him to be an heir of righteousness through faith. He was a man of appreciation!

If your purpose cannot risk extinction to honour God, where is it from? Divine purpose does not conserve what should be offered to God. Destiny makes sacrifice. It offers up scarcity by burning. When you burn something, you cannot recover it. If you have burnt your personal desires to embrace divine destiny, don't look back. If you have offered up your ambitious career in order to follow a predestined vision, don't ever regret it. In some years to come, you will be grateful that you did. No sacrifice is too much to follow God's predetermined design for your life. Whatever God has called you into, whether business, ministry, profession, etc, stay focused, and you will be victorious.

THE ORIGINAL PURPOSE

It is a proven fact that nothing is created or made without purpose. This reality of life is true whether in the physical or spiritual realm. Purpose is the reason for creation. For any painting created by an artist, there is a statement behind the oil. The potter sees the end before mixing the clay. In the same vein, God defined the purpose of man before making him. He saw the revelation before embarking on the genesis. The revelation is the expected outcome of creation.

When God created man, He revealed a statement of purpose. This statement is a statement of blessing and destiny, which is responsible for guiding a man's vision and fulfilment on earth.

Genesis 1:28-31 (New King James Version)
'Then God blessed them, and God said to them, "Be fruitful and multiply; fill the earth and subdue it; have dominion over the fish of the sea, over the birds of the air, and over every living thing that moves on the earth." And God said, "See, I have given you every herb that yields seed which is on the face of all the earth, and every tree whose fruit yields seed; to you it shall be for food. Also, to every beast of the earth, to every bird of the air, and to everything that creeps on the earth, in which there is life, I have given every green herb for food"; and it was so. Then God saw everything that He had made, and indeed it was very good. So the evening and the morning were the sixth day.'

When God blessed *'them'*, it was only Adam that was in existence. In spite of that, God saw the whole of humanity in the seed of Adam, and pronounced a divine blessing and destiny on *'them'*. So, the past, present, and generations unborn are partakers of that divine blessing pronounced by Deity. That original pronouncement is man's original purpose in life.

To tap into the original purpose, it is necessary to understand its substance. After pronouncing the blessing, God made another vital statement. He said, *'See, I have given you.'* It means, the key to enjoying the benefits of the blessings showered on you, is to see what you have been given. If you can see it, you can eat it. God did not just ask man to see, He further said, *'See, I have given you EVERY.'* So, how much you see is how much you eat. If you see some things, you will eat some things, but if you see everything that you've been given, you will benefit from everything. To prove that it is possible to see everything, God showed us how to see. From the above passage, it was written that, *'God saw everything that he made'*. If He saw everything, we can also see everything, because we are made in His image. When we look, we must see our divine purposes being *'indeed very good'*. If we can see everything with the intention of *'being very good'*, we will also obtain the results that are very good.

FRUITFULNESS

Fruitfulness is the production of good results, benefits, and profitability. It is also the production of abundance of growth and increase. Fruitfulness is connected to flourishing, success, prosperity, fertility, and procreativity.

Psalm 92:12-15 (New King James Version)
'The righteous shall flourish like a palm tree, he shall grow like a cedar in Lebanon. Those who are planted in the house of the LORD

shall flourish in the courts of our God. They shall still bear fruit in old age; they shall be fresh and flourishing, to declare that the LORD is upright; He is my rock, and there is no unrighteousness in Him.'

The palm trees are multifunctional. They provide oil, fats, husks for making ropes and mats, fuel, charcoal, juice, milk, sugar, ice creams, wine, and vinegar. They are also useful in construction and for making furniture, brooms, weapons, wax, capes, baskets, raffia, hats, hammocks, piassava, etc. The uses of a palm tree are so numerous, and that qualifies it for flourishing.

Cedars are evergreen coniferous trees growing up to 40 meters or 130 feet tall. They have a trunk that is about 2.5 meters in diameter. They are among the biggest trees in the world. Their uses are also diverse. Apart from being one of the hardest woods useful in construction, their oil is known to have many uses in natural medicine.

Those who follow the original divine purpose are righteous. Righteousness makes you flourish like the palm tree and grow like the cedar in Lebanon. When God plants you, you are bound to flourish.

Old age does not extinguish divine purpose. Fruitfulness is not tied to youthfulness, but to righteousness. Your destiny is independent of your age, if you depend on God. No righteous person has the right to be unfruitful or stale. No person who embraces divine purpose has the audacity to be unproductive. It is against the law of destiny to wither when you're planted in the courts of God.

Proverbs 8:19 (New King James Version)
'My fruit is better than gold, yes, than fine gold, and my revenue than choice silver.'

The quality of fine gold is measured in millesimal fineness. It is a system denoting the purity of platinum, gold, and silver alloys by parts per thousand. The purest type of gold in the market has 999.99 of fineness. 24 carat gold has a fineness of 999. It means that 24 carat gold has 99.9% purity. No matter how fine gold may be, the fruit of the righteous is purer, better, and possesses higher qualities than it. Fruitfulness can buy the finest gold, but the most expensive gold cannot buy fruitfulness.

Just like gold, the most expensive silver has a fineness of 999.99, yet, the revenue of divine purpose far exceed its gains. So, when God said 'be fruitful', the fruitfulness that He was pronouncing is not just the increase of plants, herbs, and the offspring of sexual or asexual reproductions. Fruitfulness is wholesome. It is spiritual, mental, and physical. If you base fruitfulness only on the physical dimension, fine gold will be your goal, and perhaps become your god. But if you understand the depth of procreativity, your goal will be the goal of achieving a God-given destiny.

2 Kings 19:30 (New King James Version)
'And the remnant who have escaped of the house of Judah shall again take root downward, and bear fruit upward.'

Your depth determines your height. Your depth also determines your manifestation. To go upward, your root must go downward. If you must be fruitful, you will need to dig very deep. When you dig deep, you will become very productive. To hold a huge edifice, a foundation must be very strong. A strong foundation is measured by its depth. What will keep the remnant alive is their ability to be fruitful. If they bear no fruit, they will die of starvation. Starvation exposes the remnant to the enemies. When you're exposed, you will be captured.

A deeper angle to fruitfulness is that it must be continuous, repetitive, perpetual, uninterrupted, and eternal. The Bible says, *'And the remnants who have escaped of the house of Judah shall AGAIN take root downward, and bear fruit upward.'* When the word *'again'* is used in a statement, it means that the action should occur more than once. Fruitfulness is not a one off activity, it is a lifetime endeavour. You're not fruitful because you want to be, you're fruitful because you are endowed to be. To those who understand divine purpose, fruitfulness is a nature, because it came with creation. You don't struggle to do something that was created to be part of you. For example, no one struggles to be hungry. It is a natural phenomenon.

THE THREE STAGES OF FRUITFULNESS

The three stages of fruitfulness are:

- The seed stage
- The sowing stage
- The harvest stage
-

1. THE SEED STAGE

In the seed are the concept, impression, offspring, and posterity. The seed is the fertilised and mature ovule carrying the embryo of the future. It is the part of a plant that has the ability to reproduce.

In fruitfulness, there are different types of seed according to the Bible. There is the seed of the woman, the Seed of Abraham, the seed of thoughts or ideas, the seed of righteousness, the seed of talents, the seed of offerings, the seed of the word, etc. What you sow is what you reap.

If we don't understand the concept of the seed, we cannot understand the concept of fruitfulness. If we narrow down fruitfulness to making babies, we will also narrow down divine purpose. You cannot flourish without knowing what should flourish. Flourishing is very versatile. As you flourish in producing babies, you also need to flourish in producing creative ideas, talents, giftings, inventions, innovations, research, science and technology, business excellence, etc. It is mediocrity to concentrate on an integral part of procreativity. You can't manifest until you explore everything that has been freely given to you divinely. To fulfil the work of the ministry, all-round fruitfulness cannot be negotiated.

Galatians 6:7-10 (New King James Version)
'Do not be deceived, God is not mocked; for whatever a man sows, that he will also reap. For he who sows to his flesh will of the flesh reap corruption, but he who sows to the Spirit will of the Spirit reap everlasting life. And let us not grow weary while doing good, for in due season we shall reap if we do not lose heart. Therefore, as we have opportunity, let us do good to all, especially to those who are of the household of faith.'

The word *'Whatever'* means everything or anything, no matter what. You cannot reap more than what you have sown. If you sow only the seed of babies, you cannot expect the fruit of ideas and inventions to manifest. What you will simply have are babies. If you reap the fruit of what you have not sown, then, the law of sowing and reaping has been broken. This is impossible. If you sow to the flesh, you cannot reap eternal fruits. No one can mock God by using the name of Jesus to claim the fruit they have not sown. You cannot claim good results from poor preparations by simply saying, *'in Jesus' name'*. That is an insult to the God of diligence. Sowing is not God's responsibility, it is yours. His responsibility was to make the law that whenever you sow, there must be fruit. The mandate has already been declared, it is your actions that will put you in the position of manifestation. Your future, destiny, purpose, and wealth are in your seed. When you sow it, you will reap it.

Again, we must understand that sowing the seed is doing good. In the above passage, the Bible says, 'And let us not

36

grow weary while doing good, for in due season we shall reap if we do not lose heart.' If you do not sow the seed, you are not doing good. James 4:17 says, 'Therefore, to him who knows to do good and does not do it, to him it is sin.' Unfruitfulness is sinfulness. Jesus cursed the fig tree because of unfruitfulness. If you are not productive, you're an embarrassment to the Kingdom of heaven.

When we think of seeds, we must also think of the following:

The viability of the seed: my wife told me a story of her Uncle who was a farmer. During a harvest season, he would sort out the best crops for preservation. The purpose of preserving those viable crops was not for consumption, he prepared them for another planting season. The non-viable ones were to be eaten. His action always angered the children in the house, because they felt that they were entitled to eat the best. But as a farmer, he understood the relevance of viability, because what you sow is what you reap. If you sow viability, you will reap viability, and vice versa.

Viability is having the ability to grow, expand, and develop. Not all seeds are viable. If you don't sort the seed before planting, your harvest may not produce the best fruits.

Matthew 7:17 (New King James Version)
'Even so, every good tree bears good fruit, but a bad tree bears bad fruit.'

There is no good tree without a good seed, and no bad tree without a bad seed. It is the seed that determines the fruit. The viability of the seed is the quality and healthiness of what is being sown. The measure of the quality of your commitment, talent, giftings, time, righteousness, money, etc will manifest in your fruit. If you pretend to man, your fruit can't pretend because your fruit will expose your identity.

Galatians 6:7 (New King James Version)
'Do not be deceived, God is not mocked; for whatever a man sows, that he will also reap.'

A mock fruit is an imitation; it is counterfeit, fraudulent, caricature, and substitution. Making an attempt to reap what you have not sown is an attempt to defraud God. If you're carrying the fruit of a seed that you've not sown, you're either a thief, or that fruit is a counterfeit. A counterfeit product cannot stand the test of fire and time.

Preservation of the seed: seasons and time determine the sowing period. When it is not time for planting, the seed must be preserved. Preservation keeps the seed alive, safe, conserved, and sustained. A fruitful-minded person knows that there are birds whose appetites long after his seed. If he does not protect what he has, predators will eat up his future. Apart from birds, there are weather conditions that are also unfavourable to your seed. To shield your seed, you must create a suitable condition that will maintain its original structure. Besides natural factors, carelessness can cause injury to your seed, thereby making it less viable. Caution must be the watch word in preservation.

In life, if you cannot create a seed bank, you will lose your destiny. A seed bank has facilities that preserve a wide variety of seeds in an underground cavern. The storage rooms are kept at temperatures that deter spoilage. The conditions in a seed bank ensure low metabolic activities and delay the seed from ageing.

The seed of the woman, righteousness, talents, giftings, etc require preservation. If you don't protect what you have, you will mortgage your divine purpose. There are conditions in life that will come after your seed if you are careless and uncommitted. Where you bank your seed determines its preservation. Some people have left their seeds exposed to the wrong conditions, and have ended up in regrets. The life that ends with regrets is the life whose seeds were not preserved. There cannot be continuity where the seed is dead. A dead seed is a dead destiny. A dead seed means there is no future.

There are people who are in the habit of eating up their seeds. It is foolishness to be a seed eater. It is a sign of lack of vision. Does it surprise you when people eat up their investment capitals? Some people have eaten up the destiny of their children. The resources that should be saved for a better education have been spent on expensive designer wears. When fashion eats up future, it is a disaster.

Matthew 6:19-21 (New King James version)
'Do not lay up for yourselves treasures on earth, where moth and rust destroy and where thieves break in and steal; but lay up for yourselves treasures in heaven, where neither moth nor rust destroys and where thieves do not break in and steal. For where your treasure is, there your heart will be also.'

Your seed is your treasure. Moths are insects closely related to the butterfly. There are about 150,000 to 250,000 different species that have been studied, yet, there are still thousands of them that are yet to be described. Moths are the major agricultural pests in most parts of the world. They cause severe damage to forests, fruit farms, and many economic crops.

Viable seeds are destroyed by demonic and self inflicted moths and rusts. Preserving your ministry, giftings, talent, children, righteousness, holiness, ideas, businesses, etc with God will prevent damage and wastage.

Transportation of the seed: some seeds are very small but carry great destinies. The smaller they are, the more careful you should be in transporting them. If you look down on any seed, and carry it carelessly, you may lose a great tree that will yield great fruits.

Matthew 25:44-46 (New King James Version)

'"Then they also will answer Him, saying, 'Lord, when did we see You hungry or thirsty or a stranger or naked or sick or in prison, and did not minister to You?' Then He will answer them, saying, 'Assuredly, I say to you, inasmuch as you did not do it to one of the least of these, you did not do it to Me.' And these will go away into everlasting punishment, but the righteous into eternal life."'

There is great reward hidden in small seeds. There is a great revelation to be uncovered in small ideas. There is a great destiny in the lives of the so called insignificant people. If you feed the small seed when it is hungry, water it when it is thirsty, shelter it when it is exposed, clothe it when it is naked, and visit it when it is sick or in prison, the reward you get from it will beat your imagination. But, if you ignore it, the consequences will be devastating.

Matthew 19:14 (New King James Version)

'But Jesus said, "Let the little children come to Me, and do not forbid them; for of such is the kingdom of heaven.'

There is power in little things. There is a kingdom hidden in little seeds. You must carry them with care. You must package them neatly and box them cautiously so that you won't lose a single one. If one goes missing, you may have lost a whole kingdom.

Matthew 13:3-8 (New King James Version)

'Then He spoke many things to them in parables, saying: "Behold, a sower went out to sow. And as he sowed, some seed fell by the wayside; and the birds came and devoured them. Some fell on stony places, where they did not have much earth; and they immediately sprang up because they had no depth of earth. But when the sun was up they were scorched, and because they had no root they withered away. And some fell among thorns, and the thorns sprang up and choked them. But others fell on good ground and yielded a crop: some a hundredfold, some sixty, some thirty.'

40

There are certain seeds that you can't afford to handle carelessly. As you transport such seeds for sowing, be mindful of the wayside, stony places, and thorns. Where your seed falls, is a factor that determines your fruitfulness. You may have viable seeds, but if they fall on the wrong ground, they cannot produce good fruits.

2. THE SOWING STAGE

Sowing is the scattering, implanting, propagating, and disseminating of seeds over land and earth for the purpose of growth and fruitfulness. You can't birth productivity without sowing a seed. Dying with an unsown seed negates the essence of divine purpose. Unfruitfulness is unfaithfulness, and unfaithfulness is an attitude of disobedience. No excuses are accepted in the spirit realm for making procreativity dormant.

Genesis 38:8-10 (New King James Version)
'And Judah said to Onan, "Go in to your brother's wife and marry her, and raise up an heir to your brother." But Onan knew that the heir would not be his; and it came to pass, when he went in to his brother's wife, that he emitted on the ground, lest he should give an heir to his brother. And the thing which he did displeased the LORD; therefore He killed him also.'

God kills those who deliberately refuse to sow, because they are discontinuing life. It is only God that has the power to discontinue life. If you make yourself the Omnipotent by deciding when life should end, your name will never be found in the Book of Life.

Wasting a seed is satanic. God does not condone it. He killed Onan because he wasted the seed of continuity. When you waste the seed of giftings deposited in you, you waste a productive future. Selfishness is a waster. Onan was selfish,

41

so he wasted an unborn destiny. He wasted this destiny by deliberately sowing on a ground that would not yield fruit. Sowing on infertile soil displeases God.

For every seed sown, a new life is born. For every divine gift or talent planted, a new generation emerges. If you're ignorant of the seed in you, or too lazy to plant, you're attempting to bring the earth to a standstill. When you sow, you're adding value to planet earth.

For a seed to be sown, it must go through the following stages.

The fall: every seed that is sown must fall to the ground. If there is no fall, there is no fruitfulness. Avoiding the fall is avoiding the fruit.

John 12:24 (New King James Version)
'Most assuredly, I say to you, unless a grain of wheat falls into the ground and dies, it remains alone; but if it dies, it produces much grain.'

When the word *'assuredly'* is used, it means undoubtedly, absolutely, definitely, positively, certainly, and surely. If the word *'most'* is used as an adjective to qualify *'assuredly'*, it shows how emphatic that phrase is. If Jesus says *'most definitely, I say to you'*, take that statement very seriously. It is most definite that unless a seed falls into the ground and dies, it remains self-centred.

Whatever seed you have must fall if you really want to expand. If you don't invest your seed, you will remain single. When the seed falls, it doesn't fall on the ground but into the ground. Falling into the ground makes you hidden and unknown for a while. Falling into the ground makes you unpopular, but protected. The seed in the ground cannot be preyed by birds and insects, or be swept away by erosion. It may not be comfortable being in the ground because of limited oxygen and light, but the essence is to create death.

The death: a fall becomes irrelevant if you are not willing to die. If a seed is thrown into the ground, and does not die, that seed can never be fruitful. There is life in dying. Death is the prerequisite to abundance. It is expedient for production. When you die, you lose self. Humbleness is an investment principle. It is the death that yields much grain.

Romans 5:8 (New King James Version)
'But God demonstrates His own love toward us, in that while we were still sinners, Christ died for us.'

It takes love to die. It takes love to sow, so that others can benefit from your fruit. God sowed the Seed of Abraham; Jesus Christ, so that humanity can reap salvation.

The growth and pruning: growth is an expansion, increase, and development. For growth to be purposeful, it must be pruned. Pruning involves elimination, exclusion, shaping, docking, and thinning. When you prune, you cut off superfluous or undesired twigs, branches, or roots. In pruning, you trim, get rid of, remove and clear away anything that may be increasing but impeding purpose. Pruning is painful. Pruning sheds the sap. The bleeding that comes from pruning is for the purpose of productivity.

John 15:1-2 (New King James Version)
'I am the true vine, and My Father is the vinedresser. Every branch in Me that does not bear fruit He takes away; and every branch that bears fruit He prunes, that it may bear more fruit.'

Every idea must be pruned to get the best out of it. No one wears raw gold; it must be refined. The process of refining is very hurtful. It takes the right character to withstand the heat of purification. Pruning increases fruitfulness. When God prunes you, your fruits will endure.

The harvest: a harvest is a supply of anything gathered at maturity and then stored. It is the season when ripened crops are gathered. Harvest is a fruition and accumulation of yields and produce.

Ecclesiastes 3:1-2 (New King James Version)
'To everything there is a season, a time for every purpose under heaven: time to be born, and a time to die; a time to plant, and a time to pluck what is planted.'

Plucking what is planted is a huge responsibility. Fruitfulness will be wasted if the skills of harvesting are missing. A good sower cannot harvest alone because his yields are plenteous. To harvest therefore, you need skilful and committed labourers.

Matthew 9:37-38 (New King James Version)
'Then He said to His disciples, "The harvest truly is plentiful, but the labourers are few. Therefore pray the Lord of the harvest to send out labourers into His harvest."'

Not every worker is a labourer. Workers are many, labourers are few. Workers come for the money, labourers come for the passion. Workers know too much, labourers are willing to learn. Workers are corporate; labourers can do any dirty job without complaining. Workers earn salaries, labourers earn wages. Workers, in harsh weather conditions will dodge work; labourers will show up under any condition. Workers are paid monthly, labourers are paid daily. Workers are not easily fired, labourers are careful not to make errors because they can easily be shown the way out.

Are you a worker or a labourer? Labourers are target-driven, committed, humble, and appreciative for the opportunity to make stipends. When you hire a worker that has the mentality of a labourer, you can never regret it.

It is only God who sees the hearts of men that knows whether a man is a labourer or a worker. During your harvest time, the key to having the right people is asking God to be your human resources agent. Labourers are very high in demand, yet, very small in number. If you understand that the harvest actually belongs to God, you will pray the Lord of the harvest to send you labourers. The Lord can only send labourers into *'His harvest'* not *'Your harvest'*.

Luke 12: 16-20 (New King James Version)

'Then He spoke a parable to them, saying: "The ground of a certain rich man yielded plentifully. And he thought within himself, saying, 'What shall I do, since I have no room to store my crops?' So he said, 'I will do this: I will pull down my barns and build greater, and there I will store all my crops and my goods. And I will say to my soul, "Soul, you have many goods laid up for many years; take your ease; eat, drink, and be merry."' But God said to him, 'Fool! This night your soul will be required of you; then whose will those things be which you have provided?'

The rich man was full of *'I'* and *'My'* without realising that the harvest belongs to God. No individual can personalise a harvest, it is God that gives the increase.

The lesson to be learnt from the rich man is his understanding of storage. When fruitfulness comes, your ability to increase the capacity of your storehouse is expedient; maintaining a rigid capacity results in wastage. When there is an increase, invest in expanding your territory. If you need to retrain in order to reposition, do it. You can't carry a small barn mentality in a big harvest. The purpose of expanding your territory must be for the reason of reinvesting. If like the rich man, you tell your soul to take its ease, eat, drink, and be merry, you will end up wasting the seeds of investment. Wasters are fools. They gather so much but end up with nothing. They eat up their past, present, and future in just a few years. There is no tomorrow for those who eat up their turnovers. There is no continuity for people who consume all the profits without setting aside a certain percentage for reinvestment. Heaven backs up reinvestment in every capacity. Reinvestment is fruitfulness.

MULTIPLICATION

Multiplication is a blessing that accompanies divine purpose. It is one of the fulfilments of destiny. It is a successor to fruitfulness. When a person becomes fruitful, he must advance to the level of multiplication. The processes of multiplying, is the act of reinvesting fruitfulness. Fruitfulness produces more seeds, while multiplication replants them.

To multiply means:

- To cause to become many.
- Having many folds, many times as great in number.
- To increase in amount, number, or degree.
- To breed or propagate.
- To combine.
- To increase in number by reproduction, procreation, or natural generation.

Multiplication can be additional, exponential, or geometric. Addition multiplication is the commonly known type. It is also the lowest form of multiplication. If you settle for this type of multiplication, you will increase but not fully maximise your potentials. Geometric progression is a type of multiplication that gives you an infinite result. There is no end to its fruitfulness. That is the type of blessing that God pronounced on man. Divine purpose does not accept a multiplication that has limitation. Don't just multiply, multiply geometrically. God's mathematics is very geometric in nature. He said, 'One will chase one thousand, and two, ten thousand'. That multiplication is completely out of this world. It even surpasses geometric progression. So brethren, never settle for less, especially when there is more up there.

HOW TO MULTIPLY

The principle of multiplication is dissemination. Dissemination is the scattering and wide spreading of seeds for the purpose of sowing. When you disseminate, three things happen; you promulgate extensively, broadcast, and disperse. Promulgation is an open declaration, publishing, formal proclamation, or putting a thing into operation. Broadcasting means the casting or scattering abroad over an area, as in the sowing of a seed. Dispersion is the driving or sending off in various directions. Dispersion dispels and scatters seeds out of sight.

Multiplication takes fruitfulness to the next level. God's blessings are graded in levels. Depending on the type of blessing, the dimensions could be in threes, fives, and sevens. If the purpose of a blessing is resurrection, the levels could be in threes or eights. If it is for favour, it is definitely fives, and if for perfection, it comes in sevens. God is a God of numbers. Never settle at the foot of a blessing until you get to the top. The top is the purpose fulfilled.

Fruitfulness provides more seeds for sowing. It is the key to multiplication. Multiplication exposes your giftings, and makes the end users appreciate you. It is the medium to creating wealth. When you multiply your seeds, you will multiply your earnings. Your income is in your multiplication. Your divine provision is in your dissemination. If you do not disseminate, you will degenerate. Degeneration is a call for poverty. Multiplication is an invitation to prosperity.

In disseminating your seeds, you must:

Step out of your comfort zone: you can't multiply if you have a small barn mentality. A small barn mentality is a comfort zone mentality. It is an attitude that ends up in just being fruitful. To step out of your comfort zone, you must be bold, and be ready to showcase what you have. You must be ready to face the harsh conditions of sowing in different weathers, and the criticisms that come with it.

See the bigger picture: if the picture in your mind is not bigger than that of fruitfulness, recreate it. You can recreate it by meditating on relevant scriptural passages, and reading inspirational books that are based on biblical teachings. The picture in your mind must be the bigger picture. You can't see a small fish and catch a shark. If you don't have an expansive mind, you can't have an expansive heart. It is your sight that moves obstacles, therefore, it must see clearly and behold bigger things.

Cross boundaries and territories: to multiply, you must be ready to possess the camps of your enemies. The promise land is not an empty land. It contains giants. If you don't have the mindset of a giant killer, remain where you are. When you cross boundaries, be ready for a fight. The occupants of where you're heading to don't give up easily. If you're not a patient and persistent fighter, you cannot survive the battle of multiplication.

Psalm 16:6 (God's Word)
'Your boundary lines mark out pleasant places for me. Indeed my inheritance is something beautiful'.

When God marks out pleasant places for you, it is your responsibility to take the land by force. If you don't, your flourishing will remain theoretical.

Do not look down on your seed: with fives loaves of bread and two fishes, Jesus fed five thousand men. His disciples saw impossibilities, but He saw abundance. When His disciples looked down on what was available, Jesus saw multiplication coming out of the limited provision.

Job 8:7 (New King James Version)
'Though your beginning was small, yet your latter end would increase abundantly.'

If you have the right character, your latter end will always be better than your beginning. It is not an offence to have a small beginning, if the latter end increases abundantly.

48

Zechariah 4:10 (New King James Version)
'For who has despised the day of small things? For these seven rejoice to see the plumb line in the hand of Zerubbabel. They are the eyes of the LORD, which scan to and fro throughout the whole earth.'

Small things are dangerous; don't ever despise them. If you despise a mustard seed, you will be in danger of missing out on some very important medicinal nutrients. It is a little leaven that leavens the whole loaf of bread. If you ignore yeast, you can also forget about fermentation.

<u>Be thankful for the seeds:</u> before feeding the five thousand men, Jesus looked up, and gave thanks. He did not complain about the quantity of the food. The major key to multiplication is thanksgiving. You must appreciate the One who gives seeds to the sower. Lack of appreciation is a call to poverty. With people's words and thoughts, they invite curses to themselves. If you are grateful for those children that God has given to you, you must not rain curses, abuses, or pronounce any negative word upon them. Appreciation does not swear. If you're grateful for the ministry, business, giftings, and talents that God has embedded in you, you must keep thanking God for them. When you give thanks, you're opening the door of abundance and new ideas. Thankful people receive divine help for destiny fulfilment. Thankful people, after feeding five thousand men, have leftovers of twelve baskets. For ungrateful people, nothing is ever enough.

2 Timothy 3:1-5 (New King James Version)
'But know this, that in the last days perilous times will come: for men will be lovers of themselves, lovers of money, boasters, proud, blasphemers, disobedient to parents, unthankful, unholy, unloving, unforgiving, slanderers, without self-control, brutal, despisers of good, traitors, headstrong, haughty, lovers of pleasure rather than lovers of God, having a form of godliness but denying its power. And from such people turn away!

49

Being unthankful is perilous. It is one of the signs of the last days. Perilous means involving grave risks or full of grave risk, hazards, and danger. Being perilous is synonymous to threat, treachery, precariousness, vulnerability, uncertainty, and unhealthiness. When you're unthankful, you're inviting a grave risk, hazard, and danger.

When you make an unthankful person a friend, you're disobeying God. The above passage says, 'And from such people turn away'. You should not only avoid them, tell them to avoid you. Turning away is a two way method; 'I turn away from you or you turn away from me'. You must turn away because ungratefulness is infectious. If you live with ungrateful people, in a little while, you will stop appreciating God for the 'little' things. Be grateful. Gratefulness makes you great. It increases you in every dimension. It opens double doors for you.

Be hardworking: hardwork does not kill, it is laziness that does. In creating the world and its inhabitants, God spent six out of seven days working. Spending 85.71% of the time working and 14.29% resting is a good example for us to follow. The most difficult and time consuming profession to be is managing your giftings, talents, business, calling, and ministry. If you understand what your divine purpose is, you will realise that there is no night or day, opening or closing hour. Most times, you even forget to eat. In the course of writing this book, I can't remember how many times my cup of tea went cold. I hardly sleep, because I'm consumed with a passion for what I do.

Employers hardly go for lunch breaks, it is employees that do. If you want to multiply, you must spend multiple times working. If you don't work extremely hard, your dreams, visions, divine purpose, and expectations will die.

Proverbs 10:4 (New King James Version)
'He who has a slack hand becomes poor, but the hand of the diligent makes rich.'

A slack hand is an inelastic hand. An inelastic hand is a hand that cannot stretch. It is a hand that is at a breaking point. When a rubber is slack, it becomes unfit for purpose. Slackness is laziness, excuses, and complaints. A slack hand is a waste to its generation. A slack hand milks the society, but contributes nothing. A slack hand causes economic crunch. A slack hand tells lies, and robs other people in order to survive. A slack hand deceives the government to claim disability benefits, where there is no disability. A slack hand is spiritually, mentally, and physically asleep. Slackness is poverty. The more poverty eats, the hungrier it becomes. It is like a graveyard that is never tired of consuming dead bodies.

A diligent hand is the hand of creativity. It makes things that produce wealth. Societies depend on diligent hands. Diligence is hard work. It is never short of positive ideas. Diligence never stops dreaming. Diligence is productivity.

SOME SCRIPTURAL EXAMPLES OF MULTIPLYING

The scriptures illustrate examples of multiplying in three dimensions; spiritual, mental, and physical.

Multiplying man: Human resources is the best asset that the world has, and will ever have. Among all creations, man has the most developed brain. When God finished creating, he saw that His creations were good, but gave man the opportunity and blessing to make it better. God had and still has the ability to make an excellent world from the onset, but he left that challenge for man. The multiplying of man on the face of the earth has given birth to immense development.

Genesis 6:1 (New King James Version)
'Now it came to pass, when men began to multiply on the face of the earth, and daughters were born to them.'

51

When men multiplied, science and technology also did. The building of the tower of Babel is a good example of how the early men were vast in the art and science of development.

Multiplying animals, plants, and grains: Animals are very resourceful. They are sources of transportations, mechanised farming, food, scientific research, clothing, environmental protection, etc. They form one of the sources of major economic growth and wealth.

Genesis 26:12-14 (New King James Version)
'Then Isaac sowed in that land, and reaped in the same year a hundredfold; and the LORD blessed him. The man began to prosper, and continued prospering until he became very prosperous; for he had possessions of flocks and possessions of herds and a great number of servants. So the Philistines envied him.'

Animals are possessions of prosperity. Their multiplication is a symbol of progress and advancement. The more your animals multiply, the higher the number of workers you hire. So, the multiplication of animals increases the level of employment, and therefore, decreases inflation. The multiplication of animals can make nations envy you.

We cannot overemphasise the significance of plants and grains to the world. They sustain life on earth.

Ezekiel 36:30 (New King James Version)
'And I will multiply the fruit of your trees and the increase of your fields, so that you need never again bear the reproach of famine among the nations.'

Farming creates great wealth. Today, some of the richest men on earth are farmers. Michelle Ferrero, one of the richest men on earth from Italy, made his billions of dollars from selling chocolates. Chocolates are made from cocoa.

Multiplying silver and gold: silver and gold are mineral resources. Mineral resources do multiply. As long as the earth remains, there can never be an exhaustion of mineral resources. It is a divine pronouncement. God has put more than enough to sustain His creations. There are lots of mineral resources on earth that are yet to be discovered. There are heavy deposits of unknown treasures sitting in the bottom of the earth. The poorest nations should realise that they are sitting and walking on unbelievable treasures that can create massive economic turnaround in their countries. God, the Father of research, can reveal to a nation that fears and acknowledges Him, the locations of overwhelming treasures.

Deuteronomy 8:13 (New King James Version)
'And when your herds and your flocks multiply, and your silver and your gold are multiplied, and all that you have is multiplied.'

Mineral resources increase in value and quantity. They can never finish. Any scientific forecast that gives a contrary opinion is a lie. God's word can never deceive. It was written before creation. The world existed in God before it was made. Therefore, God has seen the end from the beginning.

Multiplying new wine and oil: As long as the earth remains, fluidity can never dry out. Apart from the physical wine and oil, new wine is a symbol of new ideas, new information, new dreams, and new purposes. The oil gives the enablement to bring into fruition all the ideas, information, dreams, and divine purpose. Whether spiritually, mentally, or physically, new wine and oil do multiply.

Hosea 2:8 (New King James Version)
'For she did not know that I gave her grain, new wine, and oil, and multiplied her silver and gold— Which they prepared for Baal.'

Winning ideas are God-given. Manifestation of those ideas is God-enabled. A boom in the oil industry is a fulfilment of the scriptures. It is a shadow of what is going on in the spiritual realm. The Bible says, 'And it shall come to pass in the last days, says God, that I will pour out My Spirit on all flesh' His Spirit is His oil, and the oil is the anointing. Don't be surprised about what is happening in the oil sector. It reflects the present day nature in the spirit realm.

Multiplying merchants: There is a boom in trade and commerce, far beyond what has ever been. International marketing has been taken to another level. You can place an order in Africa for goods that are in China, without ever visiting China, and still get your goods shipped to you within days.

Nahum 3:16 (New King James Version)
'You have multiplied your merchants more than the stars of heaven. The locust plunders and flies away.'

No one can count the stars because of their number. If you can't count the stars, you can't count the number of business transactions that are conducted on planet earth. Stars are up, merchandise takes you up. Stars shine, merchandise makes you shine. Stars give light to others; merchandise makes you give light to people. Employment, financial resources, human resources trainings, etc create awareness. Awareness is light. When you multiply merchandise, you multiply light.

Multiplying your days: This is the fulfilment of a man's days on earth. It is not enough to live, but to live and fulfil one's days. Fulfilment brings satisfactions. It brings an eternal reward. It is what makes God tell a man, 'well done' when he stands before Him.

Deuteronomy 11:18-21 (New King James Version)
'"Therefore you shall lay up these words of mine in your heart and in your soul, and bind them as a sign on your hand, and they shall be as frontlets between your eyes. You shall teach them to your children,

speaking of them when you sit in your house, when you walk by the way, when you lie down, and when you rise up. And you shall write them on the doorposts of your house and on your gates, that your days and the days of your children may be multiplied in the land of which the LORD swore to your fathers to give them, like the days of the heavens above the earth.'

The multiplying of days is an extension and expansion of your days beyond your physical presence on earth. This means, when you die, your fulfilment becomes extended to the generations after you. This is how it multiplies. When people still enjoy you after death, your days have been multiplied. When you leave a godly legacy and goodly inheritance, your days have been multiplied. When your products and divine ideas are still conquering territories, your days have been multiplied. When you leave an equation of excellence and integrity on earth, your days have been multiplied. Success is not good, if it cannot benefit the generations after you.

Multiplying mercy, peace, and love: mercy is a compassionate or kindly forbearance shown toward an offender, an enemy, or other person in one's power. It is the discretionary power of a judge to pardon someone or mitigate punishment. Mercy shows an act of kindness and an evidence of divine favour.

Peace is a cessation of or freedom from any strife or dissension. It is also a freedom from annoyance, distraction, anxiety, or evil obsession. It is a state or condition of tranquillity or serenity.

Simply, God is love. No other definition can replace these three words. God is passionate, caring, affectionate, benevolent, kind, meek, humble, a giver, etc.

Mercy, peace, and love do multiply.
Jude 2 (New King James Version)
'Mercy, peace, and love be multiplied to you.'

Daniel 4:1 (New King James Version)
'Nebuchadnezzar the king, to all peoples, nations, and languages that dwell in all the earth: peace be multiplied to you.'

1 Peter 1:1-2 (New King James Version)
'Peter, an apostle of Jesus Christ, To the pilgrims of the Dispersion in Pontus, Galatia, Cappadocia, Asia, and Bithynia, elect according to the foreknowledge of God the Father, in sanctification of the Spirit, for obedience and sprinkling of the blood of Jesus Christ: Grace to you and peace be multiplied.'

Multiplying His word: This is an increase in revelation knowledge, prophetic utterances or declarations, visions, divine ideas, divine innovations, etc. It is a sign of blessing when God's voice continues to be heard among His people. If God is silent to a people or a nation, it is a curse. The worst famine to experience is a drought of God's word. The day you don't hear God's voice, you must begin to re-examine yourself. The day your conscience stops pricking you for a sin committed, that is the day you start dying.

Acts 12:24 (New King James Version)
'But the word of God grew and multiplied.'

Don't take it for granted when you're in an environment where the word of God grows and multiplies. The presence of the abundance of His word is a symbol of open heaven. It is a sign that the Holy Spirit is at work. The environment where His word grows and multiplies is a place of answered prayer. If you're in a ministry where God's word is scarce, please, relocate. There can't be an abundance of rain where God has shut the heavens. If you remain in a place where God is not present, you will continue to experience drought. If God is absent in a place, you should also absent yourself from that environment.

Multiplying disciples: God wants us to win more and more souls for Him. This is part of God's purpose on earth for humanity. His will is that no one should perish. Perishing is not dying in a motor accident; it is the absence of God in the life of a person. A person can be physically alive, but has perished.

Acts 6:1 (New King James Version)
'Now in those days, when the number of the disciples was multiplying, there arose a complaint against the Hebrews by the Hellenists, because their widows were neglected in the daily distribution.'

Matthew 28:19-20 (New King James Version)
'Go therefore and make disciples of all the nations, baptizing them in the name of the Father and of the Son and of the Holy Spirit, teaching them to observe all things that I have commanded you; and lo, I am with you always, even to the end of the age." Amen.'

Making disciples goes far beyond preaching to someone. When you make a product well, it becomes marketable. 'Making' goes through a lot of processes, and requires so much patience. When you make a product and sell it, you make profits. Discipleship is profitable. Your disciple is your product. Your disciple is your brand displayed on the shelf of life for potential customers to admire, appreciate, and buy. If your product does not give satisfaction to customers, there will be lots of goods returned, and refunds made. Refunds reduce profitability. Success in discipleship is divine purpose fulfilled. Making a disciple is not automatic. It's not easy to convert a goat to a sheep. It can even take a lifetime to disciple a single person. It will also take other resources including money, wisdom, character, etc. Jesus called twelve potential disciples, and ended up making eleven of them. One of them killed Him. Making disciples is a sacrifice. Never get surprised if a potential disciple plots your downfall. Discipleship is not just church attendance, it is guiding and mentoring a convert until that person also becomes a mentor. Discipleship is creating a second person like you. It is having a spiritual twin brother or sister carrying the same godly character, vision, drive, and commitment as you. A true disciple will carry on from where you stopped. A true disciple has the attitude of doing greater things, achieving more, and extending your territory. The willingness and action of a convert to expand a godly vision is the multiplication of discipleship.

Multiplying signs and wonders: A sign is a token, indication, or any object, action, event, pattern, conventional or arbitrary mark, figure, symbol, notice, direction, or warning that conveys a meaning.

A wonder is an amazement, awe, marvel, something strange and surprising, astonishment, puzzle, etc. Behind every spiritual sign, there is a wonder. Wonders dazzle human imaginations. God is full of wonders.

Exodus 7:3 (New King James Version)
'And I will harden Pharaoh's heart, and multiply My signs and My wonders in the land of Egypt.'

Signs and wonders confirm the spoken word. Where they are absent, the word is powerless. Where they are scarce, the effectiveness of God's word is limited. Signs and wonders only follow revealed knowledge, not religion. If you preach religion, you will multiply rebellion, but when you share the gospel of freedom in the Holy Ghost, signs and wonders will multiply. The message you preach is the sign you see. If your message concentrates on the outside rather than the inside, you will see carnal signs, but if you focus on the inside, the hearers will be convicted to change their outside. The signs you see are functions of the things you say. The wonders you experience are results of the signs you see. What you see has the ability to multiply. Signs are visible, never take them for granted; they can forewarn you; like the sign featuring the hand of a man rising from the sea, which indicates heavy rain. The results of signs birth overwhelming wonders.

Multiplying visions: A vision is insightful, imaginative, divine, anticipatory, vivid, and extraordinary. Visions tell the future. They speak of things to come. A vision is a man's destination from where he stands. A focus on a vision gives direction. Where a vision is absent, people stumble. A family without vision is a home without direction. A vision makes you plan, because it gives you an expectation. If you're not expecting, then you're not pregnant. If there is no conception, you cannot birth new babies. If you don't birth new babies, you're negating the blessings of multiplication. A vision gives you the drive to make preparations. A man with a vision makes purchases that are targeted towards expectations. He invests in things that point towards vision actualisation. He is never frivolous.

Hosea 12:10 (New King James Version)
'I have also spoken by the prophets, and have multiplied visions; have given symbols through the witness of the prophets.'

Visions do expand. The expansion of a vision exceeds the immediate generation. Visions are completely elastic, far beyond Young Modulus (sorry, I am talking Physics). Their expansivity is the result of their multiplication. It is God that multiplies visions, not you. Multiplication of visions is a function of obedience. Obedience makes God increase your horizon. When you act on His spoken word, you will see the bigger picture. The more you see the bigger picture, the more you walk in it. Vision is the picture of divine purpose. It is only what you see that has the tendency to multiply.

59

FILL THE EARTH

To fill means:

- To make full or put as much as can be held into.
- To occupy to the full capacity.
- To supply to an extreme degree or plentifully.
- To satisfy fully a hunger.
- To meet satisfactorily as required.

When you fill, you fill away, fill in, fill out, or fill up. Filling the earth involves every type and principle of filling. Filling the earth is a divine mandate and blessing. It is the third level of blessing pronounced on humanity. When you fill the earth, you are fulfilling divine purpose. Filling is synonymous to sufficiency, distribution, replenishment, discharge, overflow, permeation, and saturation.

Sufficiency: sufficiency is an adequacy required to fulfil purpose. It is the quantity of a supply enough to meet a need.

2 Corinthians 9:8-9 (New King James Version)
'And God is able to make all grace abound toward you, that you, always having all sufficiency in all things, may have an abundance for every good work. As it is written: "He has dispersed abroad, He has given to the poor; His righteousness endures forever."'

Sufficiency creates abundance for every good work. The key behind sufficiency is dispersion. If you disperse abroad, you will be able to provide for the poor. Provision for the poor is equated for an enduring righteousness.

Distribution: distribution means to spread throughout a space or area. A spread is a dispersion or dissemination.

1 Corinthians 7:17 (New King James Version)
'But as God has distributed to each one, as the Lord has called each one, so let him walk. And so I ordain in all the churches.'

Distribution helps you reach each one. It is a marketing principle that makes sure a product gets to every home. It is one of the ideas behind filling the earth. If you don't manage distribution properly, you're not fulfilling divine purpose. Giftings, talents, ministries, businesses, etc must be properly distributed in order for purposes to be fulfilled. If you don't walk in a skilfully managed distribution strategy, you're not pleasing God.

Replenishment: replenishment means to make full or complete again, to restock, or resupply. This is an indication that even after exhausting what has been supplied, God has given man the mandate to recreate and resupply what is missing. It is not surprising therefore, when Scientists are able to recreate certain species, or advance certain areas of technology. Those actions are a manifestation of the original blessing pronounced on man. They are a fulfilment of God's original purpose and intention for humanity. The ability to recreate is awesome. Recreating ideas, giftings, etc gives freshness to planet earth. If you can't recreate, you can't replenish. If you're not replenishing, you're just a waster. Consumers who put nothing back to earth are environmental hazards. They spend, expend, use, and plunder without replacing. If everyone has the mentality of expenditure, then one day, there will be nothing left on earth. If you're not adding value to earth, you're a disobedient creature with an unused divine mandate.

Discharge: discharging is relieving a charge, obligation, responsibility, performance, or execution. A charge is electrifying. Divine purpose is electrifying. It takes a charge to fulfil a huge responsibility. Charges are inspirational. When you discharge divine purpose, you receive divine satisfaction. When you release your giftings into action, the zeal that will drive you into fulfilment will be made available. Without discharging, you cannot fill the earth.

Overflow: when something overflows, it goes beyond its territory. An attitude of overflow is selfless and unlimited. It is a barrier breaking mentality that is fearless and unintimidated.

61

When rivers overflow, they care less about their banks.

Joel 3:13 (New King James Version)

'Put in the sickle, for the harvest is ripe. Come, go down; for the winepress is full, the vats overflow— for their wickedness is great.'

The vats can only overflow when the ripe harvest is massive. God's intention for man is to have an overflow. Overflow is a provision that's more than enough. When you overflow, you take your giftings beyond a selfish pursuit. Overflowing makes you move from scope to scope, region to region, and continent to continent.

Permeation: permeation is a penetration strategy. Where there is permeation, there may not be an easy or open access. Your ability to go through the pores to make an impact on earth requires divine wisdom. In filling the earth, you will face resistance. You will require the right skills and divine enablement to help you walk around those obstacles to manifest your destiny.

Judges 18:9-10 (New King James Version)

'So they said, "Arise, let us go up against them. For we have seen the land, and indeed it is very good. Would you do nothing? Do not hesitate to go, and enter to possess the land. When you go, you will come to a secure people and a large land. For God has given it into your hands, a place where there is no lack of anything that is on the earth."'

The position of filling the earth is a position where there is no lack of anything. The land is very good, but you must be ready to fight, because the people who inhabit the land are secure. There is a place for every one who is willing to pay the price, since the land is large. In spite of its largeness, there are people who are ready to stop you from entering. You either confront them or avoid them. Whatever strategy you adopt, make sure you penetrate. If you don't penetrate, you will remain a local champion. Your brand becomes regionalised if you hesitate or fear stronger oppositions. To spread out, you must be bold and ready to act quickly. So, arise, go hastily and possess your possessions because God has given you the land. You're responsible for taking what has been given to you.

Saturation: saturation in terms of magnetism means an utmost charge. In other words, it means to soak, impregnate, or imbue thoroughly or completely. In terms of marketing, it is the furnishing of a market with goods to its full purchasing capacity.

People who have the attitude of saturation can never be stopped by opposition. To fill the earth, you must be charged to full capacity. It is the charges that will energise you to keep firing when doubters say you can't make it.

Isaiah 27:6 (New King James Version)
'Those who come He shall cause to take root in Jacob; Israel shall blossom and bud, and fill the face of the world with fruit.'

When God becomes your root, you will blossom, bud, and saturate the earth with your fruit. Your fruit is your brand. Your brand is your ministry, product, business, talent, giftings, and whatever God has called you to do. It is possible to reach the whole earth because the blessing has already been pronounced. It was pronounced before you were born. In the blessing is the enablement for fulfilment.

HOW TO FILL THE EARTH

In filling the earth, there are certain vital inputs you require to get to your dream destination. The seeds you possess can yield unlimited fruits if you follow divine and professional principles. You can achieve the best in life, if you follow the best advice. Divine guidance plus skilful ideas give immeasurable success.

To cross boundaries, the following principles must be evident:

Understanding international marketing: international marketing is global marketing. This marketing is carried out overseas or across national borderlines. It is defined by the American Marketing Association as *'The multinational process of planning and executing the conception, pricing, promotion and distribution of ideas, goods, and services to create exchanges that satisfy individual and organizational objectives'*.

Coca-cola as an organisation is the best example for a case study on international marketing. Virtually everyone on earth has heard of Coca-Cola; majority of people have also tasted her products. Even in heaven, it is well known. This is not a blasphemy. It is the truth. Coca-cola is an organisation that has fulfilled the mandate of filling the earth. Their strategies should be a case study for any business that wants to go international.

In international marketing, there are certain factors that you must take cognisance of. You must realise that each nation has its own penetration strategies. Trade barriers differ from country to country. Therefore, to enter a market, you must be aware of;

1. Political and legal influences: your understanding of political situations, the various legal systems, and variations in trade laws will give you an advantage in penetrating the market. Although the market is the people, the government controls the policies that determine entry. If you walk into a market without prior understanding, you will end up in frustration.

2. Cultural differences: there are cultural differences from country to country. What is acceptable in the home country of a brand may not be acceptable in your target nation. You need to understand the culture of the people, and make adjustments that don't negate scriptural standards. Cultural differences such as methods of greeting, acceptable standards of dressing, respect for elders, etc vary from nation to nation.

3. Language and communication barriers: one of the first things that Joseph the dreamer did when he was taken as a slave to Egypt was to learn the language. This skill became useful in the interpretation of dreams. In assuming the position of a Prime Minister, it was easier for him to relate with the people, and issue orders and instructions. To interpret the dreams and meet the satisfactions of a target nation, understanding the language is very necessary. It makes the people have more trust in you, and also gives you a sense of belonging. For people who have problems in picking up languages, it is necessary to hire and have people around you that are adept in the language and communication of your target nation.

4. Packaging: packaging helps you to customise, standardise, or adapt your idea, product, or services to meet the demand of the people. In customising, you make the product unique to each country, but in standardisation, the same product is sold across different borders. If need be, adaptation will help you do a few modifications to meet consumer expectations.

5. Decision on entry method: to enter a market, you must decide on your strategy. The various entry strategies are exportations, licensing and franchising, contract manufacturing, management contracts, turnkey projects, or direct entry strategies. You must find out what these methods mean before deciding to penetrate the market. Find out the best method available and convenient for you, before reaching a decision.

6. Branding: branding is a kind, grade, or make, as indicated by a stamp, trademark, or the like. Sometimes, businesses change their trademarks, makes, or grades, to meet the demands of their target nations. Depending on the environment, you can either upgrade or downgrade. You should rebrand your product or idea if necessary. Never be rigid. Rebranding is a penetration strategy. That was the principle Apostle Paul adopted when he took Christianity to Athens. He used the statements of Greek philosophers to initiate the preaching of the gospel.

7. Others: other issues you must take note of are promotions, pricing, distribution, weather, foreign exchange, advertising regulations, sovereignty of the nation, improved transportation, power supply, etc.

Human resources: the best asset an employer can ever have is people. People with the right skills and commitments are great values to organisations. Having the right people to work with, is a divine provision.

Matthew 4:19 (New King James Version)
'Then He said to them, "Follow Me, and I will make you fishers of men."'

When you fish men, you fish the best skills. If a man agrees to be fished, he comes with all the right characters. If you want to fill the earth, never fish babies or women, but men. 'Men' is symbolic of maturity, not gender. Men will endure hardship and pain when the going gets rough. Men will give useful and purposeful advice. Men will face opposition without being devastated. When hiring people, never hire boys. Boys are fun lovers. They don't know what it takes to go through the flame of investment. They just come for the pay, not the praise. The praise only comes when the battle is won.

Technology: rigidity, generational gap, laidback attitude, and mental laziness prevent big dreams from going global. Technology has simplified the ease of selling yourself, ideas, products, or services to the entire world in a matter of seconds. Some people with poor attitudes see technology as disdain, instead of taking advantage of its immense benefits. Through the use of the internet, satellites, information technology, etc, you can sell your products for little or no cost. The use of social networking websites like Facebook, BlogSpot, Twitter, etc makes it easier for products to penetrate nations. The world has truly become a global village. The barriers of international marketing are gradually crumbling. You must take advantage of the open doors created by technology in order to fill the earth.

SUBDUE THE EARTH

The earth is the third planet from the sun, and the densest because it's components are closely compacted. It is the fifth largest of the eight planets in the solar system, but the largest of the solar system's four terrestrial planets. The earth involves the land, solid matters, rocks and mountains, and all its natural resources. In law, land is partly defined as any part of the earth's surface that can be owned as property and everything annexed to it, whether by nature or by the human hand. The natural resources found on earth include mineral fuels, large deposits of fossil fuels such as coal, petroleum, natural gas, etc. Other forms of natural resources found on earth include gold, diamond, platinum ores, etc.

To subdue means:

- To conquer or bring into subjection.
- To overpower by superior force or overcome.
- To bring under mental or emotional control, as by persuasion or intimidation.

- To render submissive.
- To repress.
- To bring under cultivation.

Subduing requires power, authority, and intelligence. The ability to subdue is a divine blessing. Subduing the earth is overpowering all the natural resources that it contains. If you don't conquer nature, you can't reap the benefits that come with it. Nature can be very violent if not put under control. If nature submits, it becomes very useful. It is the responsibility of man to use his divine mandate to put the forces of nature into proper use. The earth is a very complex structure. To overpower it, innovations in science and technology are essential. Subduing is not a lazy man's language. It is a language of intelligence, strength, courage, creativity, and hard work. Subduing goes beyond a word of confession, it is an action word. If you can't subdue, you can't maintain order. Maintaining order crushes arrogance and violence. If you fill the earth without subduing it, your investment will either be lost, or profits minimised. Subduing takes you to an extraordinary level, and gives you unimaginable status.

To subdue the earth, you must be objective. Objectivity comes from the acquisition of the right skills and creative thinking. It goes beyond talking. Anybody can talk, but it is the one who takes the right steps that gets the right results. If an unbeliever acquires the right skills for subduing the earth, he will get the right results. If a holy man ends his actions with positive confessions and no purposeful skill, he will remain at the level of talk.

Numbers 32:20-23 (New King James Version)
'Then Moses said to them: "If you do this thing, if you arm yourselves before the LORD for the war, and all your armed men cross over the Jordan before the LORD until He has driven out His enemies from before Him, and the land is subdued before the LORD, then afterward you may return and be blameless before the LORD and before Israel;

and this land shall be your possession before the LORD. But if you do not do so, then take note, you have sinned against the LORD; and be sure your sin will find you out.'

Subduing is possessing. No one possesses a land without fighting a war. To fight a war, you must be armed and ready to take your target. Arming yourself therefore, is the first key to subduing the earth. Your arms are your mandate, relevant skills, planning, strategies, technology, and every attribute and material useful for fulfilling divine purpose.

Crossing over is a second key to subduing. You cannot cross over by sitting and maintaining the same position. You have to make a move.

James 2:26 (The Message)
'The very moment you separate body and spirit, you end up with a corpse. Separate faith and works and you get the same thing: a corpse.'

Corpses are dead bodies and when left for a few more days, begin to decay. When corpses putrefy, they emit foul smells, and inconvenience people. You can't breathe properly in the midst of smelly corpses. This is the same scenario that occurs when a person has a divine purpose, confesses it, but does not walk in it. If your actions end in confessions, you emit a decaying smell that inconveniences heaven. It is a sin not to make a move. It irritates heaven when actions are not taken to subdue the earth. Prayer is great, actions of faith are greater. When prayer connects with movement, you're made!

The third key is that you must fight. If you don't fight you can't win. In fighting, never underestimate your opponent, and don't underestimate yourself either. The earth is powerful, but you're over-powerful. Your level of power is what makes you overpower the earth. The repeated application of your skills, divine information and enablement are what energise you to conquer. If you don't apply, you can't be employed. Timidity and cowardice always avoid a fight in the name of peace. You can't be armed, cross over, and then stand to admire the land when you should be doing some shooting. No shooting, no conquering. The earth is very resistant; to conquer you must continue to show resilience. If the blessing has been pronounced, it is your attitude that will determine your ability to occupy.

HOW MAN HAS SUBDUED THE EARTH

Man has continued to conquer the earth and overpower it in various ways. Some examples are as follows;

Science and technology: in medicine, space science, energy, engineering, communications, mineral exploration, transportation, etc, man has succeeded in overpowering the earth.

For instance, in mineral, oil, gold, diamond, and platinum explorations, high tech equipment have been designed to break through hard rocks and surfaces in order to obtain the treasures from the earth's crust. Explorations involve great skills of planning, drilling, completion, production, and extraction.

In medicine, infant mortality rates have dropped significantly. People are beginning to live healthier longer lives, as new forms of drugs and medical equipment have been discovered and developed.

In engineering, sophisticated high speed aeroplanes, trains, automobiles etc have been designed and built. Some railway tracks have been constructed under water, for example, the Channel Tunnel which is about 50 kilometres long, stretches under the sea between Folkestone in the United Kingdom to Coquelles in France.

The advent of information technology has added more zest to life. Space science, the use of satellite systems, etc have improved lives to the optimum.

Arts and culture: in music, writing, arts, sports, etc, man's creativity has subdued the earth. Between 1960-1970, The Beatles made about $1billion in record sales. J.K. Rowling, the author of Harry Potter, as at March 2010, was estimated by Forbes to be worth $1billion. Harry Potter was an idea she conceived on a train trip from Manchester to London in 1990. In 2006, a single painting titled 'No. 5, 1948' by Jackson Pollock was sold for $140 million.

Take it or leave it, ideas subdue the earth. To be the best on earth, we must look inward and think about our divine purposes in life. When you identify purpose, you will walk in divine destiny.

Leadership: Those who devise and walk in the principles of leadership control the destiny of others. Leadership controls the distribution of wealth. Leadership is power. The wealthy are subject to the leaders. Power controls wealth.

Matthew 8:9 (New King James Version)
'For I also am a man under authority, having soldiers under me. And I say to this one, 'Go,' and he goes; and to another, 'Come,' and he comes; and to my servant, 'Do this,' and he does it."'

Leadership dictates the goings and comings of the led. When leaders tell you to go, you must go, and when they say come, you must come. You will run into hot waters if you disobey.

The philosopher, social scientist, historian, and revolutionary Karl Heinrich Marx is the father of communism. No matter how controversial his ideology may be, the reality is that, it ruled almost one third of the world for many decades. His ideas subdued the eastern block, and some parts of South America.

In 1776, Adam Smith's work on, 'An inquiry into the nature and causes of the wealth of nations' laid the foundation for capitalism. Today, his idea has conquered more than half of the earth. Smith's idea has formed the basis for democracy.

There is a leader in you. You can subdue the earth with that divine leadership if you pursue divine purpose.

Religion: beliefs and religions have a wide spread effect in subduing the earth. Out of the world's estimated 6.8 billion people, between 1-1.5 billion people are Muslims, 1.8-2.0 billion are Christians; 500-900 million are Hindus.

Religion has truly conquered the earth, although the challenge has been the embrace of true religion.

James 1:26-27 (New King James Version)
'If anyone among you thinks he is religious, and does not bridle his tongue but deceives his own heart, this one's religion is useless. Pure and undefiled religion before God and the Father is this: to visit orphans and widows in their trouble, and to keep oneself unspotted from the world.'

True religion shows mercy to the helpless and lives a life of separation and purity. The life of true separation and purity can only be found in Christ. The way of Christ is the way of purity. It is spotless and undefiled.

DOMINION

Dominion is the power or right to govern and control. It is a sovereign authority and rule. Dominion gives you an exclusive right, privilege, immunity, superiority, and influence. The three dimensions of dominion are:

1. DOMINION OVER THE FISH OF THE SEA

Fish easily respond to multiplicity. When a fish breeds, it lays lots of eggs. Therefore, lots of young fish are hatched. The multiplication of fish is very rapid, making their number large. Managing multiplicity requires dominion. Divine purpose has the ability to multiply. To be able to manage divine purpose, you must learn from the management of fish. If you can account for fish, you can account for man. Some of the disciples of Jesus Christ were fishermen. He deliberately chose them because of their understanding of the principle of fish management. The ability to have dominion over fish is the key to becoming fishers of men.

Dominion over fish is necessary because:

There is wisdom in the fish.

Job 12:7-8 (New King James Version)
'But now ask the beasts, and they will teach you; and the birds of the air, and they will tell you or speak to the earth, and it will teach you; and the fish of the sea will explain to you.'

The fish has the ability to explain things. If you understand how to listen, you will receive wise information.

Fishes do listen, obey, and act as messengers.

Jonah 2:10 New King James Version)
'So the LORD spoke to the fish, and it vomited Jonah onto dry land.'

Fishes don't digest fellow messengers.

The fish was a co-messenger with Jonah. It identified him as a co-worker, and did not secrete enzymes to digest him. Instead it secured and protected him.

73

Fishes transport treasures.

Matthew 17:27 (New King James Version)
'Nevertheless, lest we offend them, go to the sea, cast in a hook, and take the fish that comes up first. And when you have opened its mouth, you will find a piece of money; take that and give it to them for Me and you.'

There is money in the mouth of the fish. If you dominate it, you will find it.

Fishes are united.

They move in groups according to their species. That is why it is easy to catch a great number of a certain species of fish.

John 21:6 (New King James Version)
'And He said to them, "Cast the net on the right side of the boat, and you will find some." So they cast, and now they were not able to draw it in because of the multitude of fish.'

When God gave man dominion over the fish of the sea, He also had other technological fish in mind. The boats, ships, submarines, and underwater mineral resources such as petroleum are all part of the fish of the sea. Inasmuch as it floats, flows, or swims, it is a fish.

If you have the capacity and ability to rule over fish, you will have the audacity to access the treasure that comes with it. Technology has made it easier for man to rule the sea. Imagine the technology behind offshore oil exploration despite the depth of the sea. The Atlantic Ocean is about 3926 metres deep, Pacific Ocean; 4282 metres deep, Indian Ocean; 3963 metres deep. Man has become the landlord of the sea because he was given the dominion to be.

The sea is a great source of economic benefit to man. Approximately 71% of the earth is covered with water. Apart from acting as a medium of transportation, they are sources of food, mineral resources, etc. The sea is also responsible for dictating weather conditions.

Dominion over the fish of the sea will empower you to deal with its environment. You have been empowered to dominate. Use it.

2. DOMINION OVER THE BIRDS OF THE AIR

A bird is formally defined as any warm blooded vertebrate of the class of Aves, having a body covered with feathers, forelimbs modified into wings, scaly legs, a beak, and no teeth, and bearing young in a hard shelled egg.

Informally, a bird is defined as an aircraft, spacecraft, and guided missiles. Dominion over the birds of the air is dominion over formal and informal birds.

A bird symbolises:

<u>Sacrifice</u>

Leviticus 14:5 (New King James Version)
'And the priest shall command that one of the birds be killed in an earthen vessel over running water.'

<u>Revealer of hidden secrets</u>

Ecclesiastes 10:20 (New King James Version)
'Do not curse the king, even in your thought; do not curse the rich, even in your bedroom; for a bird of the air may carry your voice, and a bird in flight may tell the matter.'

Awakening

Ecclesiastes 12:4 (New King James Version)
'When the doors are shut in the streets, and the sound of grinding is low; when one rises up at the sound of a bird, and all the daughters of music are brought low.'

Deliverance

Exodus 19:4 (New King James Version)
'You have seen what I did to the Egyptians, and how I bore you on eagles' wings and brought you to Myself.'

Renewal

Psalm 103:5 (New King James Version)
'Who satisfies your mouth with good things, so that your youth is renewed like the eagle's.

Provision

Matthew 24:28 (New King James Version)
'For wherever the carcass is, there the eagles will be gathered together.'

Swiftness

2 Samuel 1:23 (New King James version)
'Saul and Jonathan were beloved and pleasant in their lives, and in their death they were not divided; they were swifter than eagles, they were stronger than lions.'

Messenger

1 Kings 17:6 (New King James Version)
'The ravens brought him bread and meat in the morning, and bread and meat in the evening; and he drank from the brook.'

Beauty

Song of Solomon 1:15 (New King James Version)
'Behold, you are fair, my love! Behold, you are fair! You have dove's eyes.'

God's presence

Mark 1:10 (New King James Version)
'Then a voice came from heaven, "You are My beloved Son, in whom I am well pleased."'

Safety

Matthew 10:16 (New King James Version)
'Behold, I send you out as sheep in the midst of wolves. Therefore be wise as serpents and harmless as doves.'

Not all birds symbolise good. Some birds are carnivorous, unclean, hateful, and devourers.

Revelation 18:2 (New King James Version)
'And he cried mightily with a loud voice, saying, "Babylon the great is fallen, is fallen, and has become a dwelling place of demons, a prison for every foul spirit, and a cage for every unclean and hated bird!'

Evil birds disrespect royal meals. They put their beaks on baskets that should be honoured. If you do not show dominance over them, they will cause your death. No one should be careless with birds. If you expose your basket, they will mess up its content.

Genesis 40:17-20 (New King James Version)
'In the uppermost basket were all kinds of baked goods for Pharaoh, and the birds ate them out of the basket on my head. So Joseph answered and said, "This is the interpretation of it: The three baskets are three days. Within three days Pharaoh will lift off your head from you and hang you on a tree; and the birds will eat your flesh from you."'

Dominion helps you control, overpower, and overcome the excesses of birds. It also helps you take advantage of the benefits of good birds. Most natural birds help in the dispersal of seeds. They are agents of multiplication. Birds help in balancing nature through food chains and food webs. Some birds control the spread of insects that damage agricultural produce.

Dominion has gifted man the talent and intelligence to design and manufacture informal birds such as aircrafts and spacecrafts. One evil informal bird that man must avoid is missiles. The design of these destructive birds is an abuse of the dominion mandate.

3. DOMINION OVER EVERY LIVING THING THAT MOVES ON EARTH

No living thing should ever be taken for granted. The microscopic organisms may not be seen with the naked eyes but are of great economic importance to the world. The worst killer diseases are caused by invisible microorganisms. Also, the agents of fermentation and nitrification of soil through the process of nitrogen cycle are small living organisms. Microcosm has the ability to enhance or reduce macrocosm, depending on how it is managed. Understanding the principle of dominion will bring a man into the atmosphere to maximise divine purpose. You are not fully manifesting until you dominate. Dominance is total control. It is a hundred percent capacity utilisation. It is operating to the fullest, God's expectation for you.

Whether big or small, God has given us dominion over every living thing that moves upon the earth. He has given us authority over viruses, bacteria, fungi, parasites, and all macro organisms that live on earth. You are more powerful than any cancer causing organism or any human immunodeficiency virus (HIV). Leukaemia causing agents are under your feet.

Whatever has a name and lives on earth is subject to you. It is your responsibility to exercise your dominion mandate. You have the power to control, direct, instruct, or terminate any living thing on earth. Take advantage of what is yours NOW!

THE RENEWED PURPOSE

Renewal is the window to exhilaration, regeneration, rejuvenation, revitalisation, replenishment, stimulation, and transformation. Where there is renewal, there is a new beginning, reestablishment, restoration, and remaking. The essence of renewal is to replace the old, refurbish it, or add value to it. For any new beginning, God makes a declaration of purpose. His purpose is His intention for the new realm. His purpose gives the summary of His expectation at the end of the road.

Since the creation of the earth, there have been three new beginnings, and for each beginning, God made a declaration of purpose.

The beginning with Adam: in Adam's beginning, God blessed man, and in that blessing was fruitfulness, multiplying, filling the earth, subduing the earth, and having dominion. When Adam sinned, he lost the focus of his divine purpose on earth. As a result, his dominion mandate also evaporated. Sin evaporates blessings, and introduces curses. No one can exercise divine authority under the canopy of a curse. When authority is absent, lawlessness dominates. Anyone who steps out of the Garden of Eden steps into the wild. The wild is dangerous and purposeless. There are cannibals in the wild. You cannot plan or think creatively in the wild. The fall of man introduced the termination of divine purpose during the first beginning.

The beginning with Noah: the second beginning started with Noah, the ark builder.

Genesis 6:5-8 (New King James Version)
'Then the LORD saw that the wickedness of man was great in the earth, and that every intent of the thoughts of his heart was only evil continually. And the LORD was sorry that He had made man on the earth, and He was grieved in His heart. So the LORD said, "I will destroy man whom I have created from the face of the earth, man and beast, creeping thing and birds of the air, for I am sorry that I have made them." But Noah found grace in the eyes of the LORD.'

God destroyed man and every living thing that was on earth but spared Noah and his family. Noah formed the basis of the new world. In order for this new world to prosper and have a desired end, God pronounced a blessing on Noah and his family. That blessing was the same mandate that He declared when He created Adam. So, what Adam lost as a result of sin, Noah gained as a result of grace. Grace ushers in a new beginning.

Genesis 9:1-3 (New King James Version)
'So God blessed Noah and his sons, and said to them: "Be fruitful and multiply, and fill the earth. And the fear of you and the dread of you shall be on every beast of the earth, on every bird of the air, on all that move on the earth, and on all the fish of the sea. They are given into your hand. Every moving thing that lives shall be food for you. I have given you all things, even as the green herbs.'

In the second beginning, God restored back to man what the devil had stolen from him. Grace brings restoration. If you do not have this understanding, the devil will still make you believe that he has the authority of man. He tried to play a fast one in the temptation of Jesus Christ.

Luke 4:6 (New King James Version)
'And the devil said to Him, "All this authority I will give You, and their glory; for this has been delivered to me, and I give it to whomever I wish."'

I want you to realise that the devil is a liar and a deceiver. He is very swift in twisting the truth. A twisted truth appears like truth, but within it are semantics of deception. It is true that the devil stole the authority from Adam because the authority was enclosed in dominion. But the whole truth is that the dominion was given back to Noah. What has been given back cannot be under the custody of Satan. Since Noah found grace in the eyes of the Lord, he also found restoration. Jesus, being an embodiment of divine knowledge was not ready to get entangled in a frivolous argument, so He said, *'Get behind Me Satan'*. Right from the days of Noah, the devil has lost authority over man. What he has is the angelic power that was originally with him before his fall and the ignorance that still encompasses man. Ignorance willingly donates authority to a bully. If you don't know what you have and who you are, you will submit leadership to a subordinate. Royalty can become subject if he doesn't see the crown on his head.

The beginning with Jesus Christ: some people will ask, *'If God restored authority back to man through Noah, what did Jesus come to do on earth?'* From Adam to Noah, a blessing was only earthly. It had no spiritual dimension. When God blessed man, He said, *'Be fruitful and multiply; fill the earth and subdue it; have dominion over the fish of the sea, over the birds of the air, and over every living thing that moves on the earth'*. All of that statement does not address the spiritual realm, but only focuses on carnality; physical blessings. People who don't know Christ only end in physical blessings. The coming of Jesus Christ ushered us into the heavenly realm. It took divine purpose to the heavenly dimension. This was the intention of God before the foundation of the world. A new covenant purpose is a heavenly purpose. When heaven becomes your target, the earth will be too small for a goal. To those who believe in Jesus Christ and confess Him as their Lord and personal Saviour, divine purpose goes beyond the sky.

Ephesians 2:4-7 (New King James Version)
'But God, who is rich in mercy, because of His great love with which He loved us, even when we were dead in trespasses, made us alive together with Christ (by grace you have been saved), and raised us up together, and made us sit together in the heavenly places in Christ Jesus, that in the ages to come He might show the exceeding riches of His grace in His kindness toward us in Christ Jesus.'

In the new purpose, we are seated in the heavenly places in Christ Jesus. Walking in this divine purpose gives us a twofold blessing; the original blessing of dominion mandate and the unquantifiable blessing of being a joint heir with Jesus Christ.

Romans 8:28–30 (New King James Version)
'And we know that all things work together for good to those who love God, to those who are the called according to His purpose. For whom He foreknew, He also predestined to be conformed to the image of His Son, that He might be the firstborn among many brethren. Moreover whom He predestined, these He also called; whom He called, these He also justified; and whom He justified, these He also glorified.'

In the new realm, purpose is a calling. A calling is not restricted to the work of the ministry; it involves *'all things'*. You can be called to be a farmer, administrator, cleaner, etc. Whatever office you've been called to occupy is where your justification and glory are enclosed. If you do otherwise, you will continue to struggle with no inner and most times, outer satisfaction. Calling is predestination. You are only fulfilling divine purpose if you align with the destiny that conforms to the image of Christ. If you do not align with the Firstborn, you will continue to take a second position in life.

Jesus Christ is the summary of divine purpose. Divine purpose is far beyond the physical dimension. It is a call for the heavenly. When you embrace predestination, you receive the backing of heaven in your area of calling. Wherever you've been called to operate has it's foundation in Jesus Christ. Divine purpose is heaven's mandate. It is your portion of God's divine assignment on earth.

Colossians 1:16-18 (New King James Version)
'For by Him all things were created that are in heaven and that are on earth, visible and invisible, whether thrones or dominions or principalities or powers. All things were created through Him and for Him. And He is before all things, and in Him all things consist. And He is the head of the body, the church, who is the beginning, the firstborn from the dead, that in all things He may have the preeminence.'

The devil always hates it when you include heaven in your purpose in life. He sends some ignorant people to give you ungodly counsels. Those who are earthly don't understand what divine purpose is. Some people tell you to draw a line between secular jobs and Christianity. They make you feel like there is no connection. That is a lie from the pit of hell. God is interested in heaven, earth, visible and invisible. When heaven connects with earth, visibility with invisibility, it results in preeminence. I'm not in any way suggesting that there should not be an application of common sense. Wisdom understands boundaries.

In the Seed of Abraham or the woman was eternal divine purpose, and that purpose passed through the following stages:

Preservation: before the foundation of the earth, God knew that one day, Jesus Christ was coming to die for humanity. So, He put that Seed of the new birth in the woman. That seed carried the destiny and freedom of man from satanic imprisonment.

Genesis 3:14-15 (New King James Version)
'So the LORD God said to the serpent: " Because you have done this, you are cursed more than all cattle, and more than every beast of the field; on your belly you shall go, you shall eat dust all the days of your life. And I will put enmity between you and the woman, and between your seed and her Seed; He shall bruise your head, and you shall bruise His heel.'

85

When God made the above statement, He wasn't referring to Eve as a person. He was pronouncing the birth of Jesus Christ through Mary. When you look carefully into that scripture, you will notice that the Seed of the woman is written with a capital letter 'S' and the 'He' also starts with a capital letter 'H'. Divinity is the only being addressed with a capital letter pronoun in the middle of a sentence. God announced an eternal purpose the moment man fell. He introduced a permanent solution to what seemed an eternal predicament. When He made that statement, it didn't sound big. God does big things beginning with small things. A seed is small, but in it is the future. The Seed of the woman is the carrier of the destiny of hope, salvation, deliverance, eternal life, etc.

God introduced the Seed through a prophetic utterance. Big purposes are introduced through prophetic revelations. The Seed of purpose was hidden in man for the purpose of preservation. Man carried the Seed of divine destiny for thousands of years. That is why the devil is very envious of man. He can't decipher why God should love man so much to put Himself inside man. That is why he's out to frustrate humanity and deceive them until they neglect their divine calling.

The Seed went through years of painful preservation. Preservation is not merriment. It comes with harsh confinements. Those who work in the various seed banks all over the world understand better what I'm saying. Sometimes, seeds are stored under very low temperatures below freezing point in order to avoid internal metabolic activities. The storage of the human seed; semen, also goes through the same process.

Philippians 2:8 New King James Version)
'And being found in appearance as a man, He humbled Himself and became obedient to the point of death, even the death of the cross.'

Jesus found Himself in the appearance of man the moment God declared His intention for the salvation of man. His obedience to the point of death, even the death of the cross, began immediately after the declaration. His character of submission was already formed before His birth. The renewed purpose does not wait for manifestation before cultivating the right character. For thousands of years after God's declaration, heaven went through an unimaginable pain just to come to terms with how God Himself was to face the humiliation of death. The renewed purpose was born out of the pains of travail. This pain was not the physical bruises on Jesus Christ, but the sacrifice of enduring the trauma of waiting as a preserved Seed.

Isaiah 53:11 (New King James Version)
'He shall see the labor of His soul, and be satisfied. By His knowledge My righteous Servant shall justify many, for He shall bear their iniquities.'

The travail of a soul is a mental torture. Travail means, 'painfully difficult or burdensome work', 'pain, anguish or suffering resulting from mental or physical hardship', 'to toil or exert oneself', and 'to suffer the pangs of childbirth'.

Giving birth to a new beginning demands a sacrificial labour. Mental hardship is worse than physical labour. From the days of Adam until the death on the cross, the Godhead went through a mental travail because of the salvation of man. Seeing God hang on the cross was burdensome. The renewed divine purpose is a product of travail.

Genealogy: genealogy is descent from an original form or progenitor, lineage, or ancestry. It is a record or account of the ancestry and descent of a person, family, group, etc.

Where there is a seed, there is genealogy. It is genealogy that is responsible for the transportation of the seed from generation to generation, until its expression. People find reading genealogy boring, I used to myself, until I discovered the principle in it. There is a bundle of revelation inside genealogy. It teaches the biblical transfer process, and how a believer connects with

87

the Abrahamic covenant. If you don't understand genealogy, you won't understand your rights and privileges. It makes you proud of the finished work on Calvary. Genealogy teaches you about your line of connection to the renewed purpose.

There are two accounts of Jesus' genealogy in the Bible from the gospel according to Apostle Matthew and Saint Luke. These two accounts have been subjects of theological arguments and debates, because they appear to contradict each other. These so called 'contradictions' are deliberate because God cannot be traced to a single genealogy. No one can claim ownership of being the father or mother of God. Jesus Himself answered the question of parentage before His crucifixion.

Matthew 12:50 (New King James Version)
'For whoever does the will of My Father in heaven is My brother and sister and mother."'

Doing the will of God is the key to God's genealogy. It is the key to the parenthood, brotherhood, and sisterhood of Jesus Christ. In the true sense, if the Bible was to record Jesus' genealogy, the whole earth would not contain the books. So, both Apostle Matthew and Saint Luke were right. If you include your names and that of your family, if they're born again, you're also right. Jesus is bigger than any earthly lineage. It is even demeaning to assign Him an earthly ancestry. It was as a result of the attitude of humility that made the Holy Spirit permit two accounts of genealogy in the Bible. The reason for it was to show the process of how the word became flesh. It is also to teach man that through submission and humbleness, the spoken word can become flesh.

From the account of both genealogies, the Seed of Abraham found its way into the womb of the woman. This was the fulfilment of the statement God made when man fell. Today, the Seed of the woman is bruising the head of the serpent, while that of the serpent is bruising her heel. The kingdom of light and that of darkness are in continuous warfare. Until the last day, this fight will never stop.

Manifestation: the birth of Jesus Christ was a fulfilment of the manifestation of the Seed of Abraham. It was the birth of the eternal and divine purpose of God. In this eternal purpose, we have our own purposes.

John 1:30-31 (New King James Version)
'This is He of whom I said, 'After me comes a Man who is preferred before me, for He was before me.' I did not know Him; but that He should be revealed to Israel, therefore I came baptizing with water.'''

Even John the Baptist who was to make the way for Jesus Christ confessed that he did not know Him. John was given a divine assignment; he acted in obedience without knowing the detail. Divine purpose is a mystery. It is only God that understands the fullness and destination of a person's divine assignment.

Manifestation is a revelation of the motive behind purpose. Everything cannot make sense from the beginning until you get to the end. The reason for living is fully understood at the end. Following divine purpose makes little sense at inception.

John 1:1-2 (New King James Version)
'In the beginning was the Word, and the Word was with God, and the Word was God. He was in the beginning with God.'

The mystery of renewed purpose is that it is with God, and it is God's. If your purpose in life has a beginning with God, your end will be excellent.

1 Timothy 3:16 (New King James Version)
'And without controversy great is the mystery of godliness: God was manifested in the flesh, justified in the Spirit, seen by angels, preached among the Gentiles, believed on in the world, received up in glory.'

When your purpose becomes a mystery of godliness, it will be undaunted and undoubted. A purpose that is an object of divine interest is never controversial. A divine purpose pursued with the heart of justification will manifest in the flesh. At the end of that purpose, it will be received up in glory.

May your divine purpose manifest in the flesh, be justified in the Spirit, seen by angels, preach to unbelievers, be believed on by the world, and received up in glory in Jesus' Name. Amen.

HOW TO DISCOVER YOUR PURPOSE

Purpose is not the idea. It is the motive, reason, and intention behind the idea. Purpose is the spirit behind the letter and the heart behind a pronouncement or declaration. Purpose is not the beauty of a project, but the expected result at the end of the project. If an outcome does not match the desired expectation, purpose is not achieved.

Ecclesiastes 7:8 (New King James Version)
'The end of a thing is better than its beginning; the patient in spirit is better than the proud in spirit.'

If an expectation is pursued from the beginning in the spirit of patience, the end will be better. The end is the vision and the fulfilment of purpose. In reaching the end, you must be convinced that you're on the right road. Searching for the right road of destiny is what everyone that hasn't discovered his calling should be seriously engaged in doing. For those who have discovered theirs, they should realise that purpose is expansive. The need to search for details is paramount in divine purpose. For your end to be better than your beginning, you must know what your beginning should be.

STEPS TO PURPOSE DISCOVERY

Discovery unveils something that was covered. Discovery is an uncovering of hidden facts, truth, existence, substance, etc. When you discover, you gain knowledge and insight into that which was covered. Discovery is a revelation and disclosure that helps you notice and realise what is behind the wall.

The following steps will help you discover your purpose in life;

Go back to the beginning: the beginning is the starting point of every creature. For any wise creator, the end is seen from the beginning. The end is the reason for the beginning.

In discovering purpose, you must trace your genealogy to the starting point. Your starting point includes the day you were born, the roads you have passed through, all the occurrences and recurrences, the day you got born again, the mental and spiritual pictures you've been seeing, etc. The reason for back trace is for you to do a question and answer session. Honest and wise questions give answers to purpose discovery. If you don't know your genealogy and history, it will be difficult to know where you're going.

You must ask yourself questions about the circumstances that surrounded your birth, what was seen and said before and after birth, the issues that keep recurring, the challenges you have faced and keep facing, and the reason for those challenges. You must give an honest answer to the questions of your beginning. If you don't have all the answers, ask people who were present. If you can't get satisfactory answers from people, go to God, and He will reveal it.

Sometime ago, I saw a vision about one of my neighbours. In that revelation, I was taken back to when she was five months old. As at the time of this revelation, she was already in her mid thirties, and married with four children. During this vision, as her mother was about to breast feed her, someone came and rubbed a substance on her breast. This innocent five month old baby sucked the substance. In that vision, I saw her in her real age screaming that I should intercede for her. That night, I woke up and started doing a warfare prayer. In real life, this pretty lady has gone through untold hardships, ranging from severe marital problems to financial predicaments.

The only way you can have a new beginning is by looking into the old. The new is hidden in the old. You cannot sweep history under the carpet. History is the foundation of the present and the future.

Isaiah 46:9-10 (New King James Version)
'Remember the former things of old, for I am God, and there is no other; I am God, and there is none like Me, declaring the end from the beginning, and from ancient times things that are not yet done, saying, 'My counsel shall stand, and I will do all My pleasure,'

If God declares the end from the beginning, you must go back to the beginning to see and hear what was declared. The best way to see destiny is by going back to the starting point. On a journey, when you miss your way, and you're utterly confused, going back to the starting point makes it easier for you to redirect your route.

God said, *'Remember the former things of old'*, which means, *'Go back to history'* There are stages in life when you have to go back to history. You can't treat history shabbily and expect a bright future. Your history connects with your destination, no matter how ugly it may be. Going back affords you the privilege of changing what you don't like. The hope we have in God is that He has the ability to change and fix our beginnings, if they're ruined.

93

Isaiah 61:4 (New King James Version)
'And they shall rebuild the old ruins, they shall raise up the former desolations, and they shall repair the ruined cities, the desolations of many generations.'

Joel 2:25 (New King James Version)
'So I will restore to you the years that the swarming locust has eaten, the crawling locust, the consuming locust, and the chewing locust, My great army which I sent among you.'

If you don't know what has been eaten, you won't know what should be restored. When we look back, we will see that there are desolations of many generations. If you remain on the foundation of desolations of many generations, you won't have the divine enablement to fulfil divine purpose. But when you allow the Spirit of the Lord to come upon you, you will shine.

Develop a praying ear: praying is excellent, but praying without a listening ear makes you a wanderer. There is little difference between a prayerless person and the one who prays without listening. Divine purpose is revealed to listeners. Most often, God declares purpose using the still small voice. If your mental atmosphere is noisy, you won't be able to hear what the Spirit is saying.

Matthew 11:15 (New King James Version)
'He who has ears to hear, let him hear!'

Everybody has ears, but some are not used for hearing. There is a difference between applying an organ for what it is meant for, and a misuse or misapplication of functionality. If you cannot incline your ears to the spirit realm, you won't be able to monitor the signal in heaven's radio wavelength. Most times, the volume of the sound of this station is very low. It takes those whose antenna is fully inclined to the signal to interpret the descending messages. The spiritually deaf cannot hear what the Spirit is saying. The Spirit reveals and declares purposes regularly. If you're a hearer, you will continually hear Him mention your purpose of creation. He repeats it almost daily, and makes it the centre of your focus. You sleep and wake up with it.

The still small voice is a process whereby God speaks through the voice of your spirit. When a man gets born again, it is the spirit of man that does, not his mind or physical body. It is that spirit that communes with God. Just like the physical body, the human spirit has all the designs of man. When God speaks to you, your spirit will pick up the information, and transfer it to your mind. Sometimes, you will think it is your mind that is speaking; meanwhile, it's a message from your spirit. On certain occasions, you have noticed an immediate manifestation of what you thought was a product of your mind. When you begin to notice such manifestations, develop that hearing method by obeying the instructions. The more you obey, the clearer you hear. Sometimes, you have an inner feeling that something is not right. Somehow, before the end of that day, a phone call comes in that settles your inner suspicion. That is an indication of the voice of your spirit.

God speaks majorly through the voice of your spirit. If you know how to be still and listen, you will avoid lots of errors, and walk in divine purpose. When your inner feelings continue to disturb you over an issue, respond quickly. Divine purpose is communicated mainly through your inner witness.

Be a witness bearer: divine purpose is revealed to witness bearers.

Revelation 1:1-2 (New King James Version)
'The Revelation of Jesus Christ, which God gave Him to show His servants—things which must shortly take place. And He sent and signified it by His angel to His servant John, who bore witness to the word of God, and to the testimony of Jesus Christ, to all things that he saw.'

The book of Revelation went through two stages; God gave the revelation to Jesus Christ, and Jesus gave it to His servants through John. Eternal purpose was revealed to Jesus Christ, and Jesus revealed it to the church using Apostle John as a conduit. The revelation of divine purpose is not directly to man, but through Jesus Christ. Any purpose that is not revealed through Jesus Christ is either self ambition or satanic.

The key to obtaining divine purpose revelation from Jesus Christ is being His witness. For Jesus and the Holy Spirit to receive revelation from God the Father, they have to act on the principle of witnessing.

Revelation 1:5 (New King James Version)
'and from Jesus Christ, the faithful witness, the firstborn from the dead, and the ruler over the kings of the earth.'

Romans 8:16 (New King James Version)
'The Spirit Himself bears witness with our spirit that we are children of God, and if children, then heirs—heirs of God and joint heirs with Christ, if indeed we suffer with Him, that we may also be glorified together.'

If you're not a witness bearer, you cannot receive revelations. Revelations are hidden secrets of things to come. Divine purpose is a secret of things to come. It will be revealed to you, when you bear witness of Jesus Christ. A witness sees, hears, and knows by personal presence or perception. He is someone who was there when the action took place. He saw it, heard it, felt it, beheld it, etc.

1 John 1:1–4 (New King James Version)
'That which was from the beginning, which we have heard, which we have seen with our eyes, which we have looked upon, and our hands have handled, concerning the Word of life— the life was manifested,

and we have seen, and bear witness, and declare to you that eternal life which was with the Father and was manifested to us— that which we have seen and heard we declare to you, that you also may have fellowship with us; and truly our fellowship is with the Father and with His Son Jesus Christ. And these things we write to you that your joy may be full.'

A revealed purpose borne out of witnessing makes other people's joy to be full. Purpose is never hidden from witness bearers. Witness bearers are never devoid of joy. Divine information is never hidden from witness bearers. The future is never hidden from witness bearers. Those who stand on the truth until it happens are witness bearers. Those who are never ashamed of the gospel of Jesus Christ are witness bearers. Those who win men to our Lord Jesus Christ are witness bearers. Can I have a witness?

Prayer and fasting: you can operate in a ministerial call, yet, not be in a place of purpose. In a call, there is positioning. If you're not in the right position, you will be wasting your time doing other people's work.

Acts 13:1-3 (New King James Version)
'Now in the church that was at Antioch there were certain prophets and teachers: Barnabas, Simeon who was called Niger, Lucius of Cyrene, Manaen who had been brought up with Herod the tetrarch, and Saul. As they ministered to the Lord and fasted, the Holy Spirit said, "Now separate to Me Barnabas and Saul for the work to which I have called them." Then, having fasted and prayed, and laid hands on them, they sent them away.'

Barnabas and Saul were prophets and teachers. They were doing very well in Antioch. Everything seemed to be alright. During prayer and fasting, the Holy Spirit revealed that they were not in their place of purpose. Doing well is not good enough. Being where God wants you to be is purpose.

Fasting and prayer causes a separation. This separation is a filtration and purification. Unwanted substances are removed during filtration and purification. Impurities are taken off when a person undergoes separation. During fasting, the Holy Spirit always speaks. When He speaks, He declares divine purpose. This divine purpose may be different from your current status or position. Your current status may be popular and honourable but if it is not divine, it is not designed.

1 Chronicles 4:9-10 (New King James Version)
'Now Jabez was more honorable than his brothers, and his mother called his name Jabez, saying, "Because I bore him in pain." And Jabez called on the God of Israel saying, "Oh, that You would bless me indeed, and enlarge my territory, that Your hand would be with me, and that You would keep me from evil, that I may not cause pain!" So God granted him what he requested.'

Being honourable may be different from being blessed indeed. Being honourable is good; being blessed indeed is excellent. An 'indeed blessing' is divine purpose fulfilled.

Jabez, in spite of his position cried to God for a real fulfilment. He yelled for an inner hunger to be satisfied. He did not allow his earthly position to fool him.

Consistently waiting upon God reveals a lot to us. If you don't burn out, you can't know more. Fasting subjects the body so that your spirit can hear what the Father of all spirits is saying. If you can't climb the mountain, you can't ascend into the heavenly. It is those who ascend that hear mysteries. There is no way on earth that you can have the roadmap to destiny without fasting and prayer. If you cannot fast, you will be a fad. When you're a fad, you will easily fade away.

Prophetic words and calling: a call is an invitation to duty and responsibilities. When there is a call, there must be a separation. Prophetic words reveal a call. In prophetic words,

God may speak to you directly, or use another person to communicate the message to you. Either way, there will be a confirmation. Confirmation helps you double check the prophetic message if it is true or not. Confirmation comes in form of a repeated revelation to you or to an entirely different person who was not involved in the first revelation.

Luke 2:36-38 (New King James Version)
'Now there was one, Anna, a prophetess, the daughter of Phanuel, of the tribe of Asher. She was of a great age, and had lived with a husband seven years from her virginity; and this woman was a widow of about eighty-four years, who did not depart from the temple, but served God with fastings and prayers night and day. And coming in that instant she gave thanks to the Lord, and spoke of Him to all those who looked for redemption in Jerusalem.'

Prophetic words expose divine revelations, destinies and purposes. When they are spoken, they follow the process of confirmations from independent prophets. Any prophetic message must agree with the scriptures. If it doesn't, it is not from God. God does not contradict His word. The Bible is the word of God. He cannot say one thing in the Bible and another thing through a prophet. Any prophecy that does not agree with the Bible is false and satanic.

The birth of Jesus Christ was declared thousands of years before His manifestation. Over the years, there were series of confirmations. When He was born and at His dedication, there were also confirmations. All the confirmations agreed with what was originally written concerning Christ in the Bible.

When you receive a prophetic message from a prophet, check it out from the scriptures, wait on God concerning it, and He will give you a confirmation. Confirmation either ratifies or rectifies the message.

Passion and inner drive: passion is an ardent love or affection for an object, concept, or pursuit. It is a state of mind and strong emotion affected by something external such as perception, desire, and drive. A drive makes you carry vigorously through, and keeps you going. It is a force that causes you to move, in spite of pains and distress.

Passion unveils our deep interest toward something. A deep selfless interest toward a thing is divine purpose revealed. The strong inner urge towards a certain skill, creativity, calling, profession, discipline, etc, is an indication of real purpose.

2 Kings 10:16 (New King James Version)
'Then he said, "Come with me, and see my zeal for the LORD." So they had him ride in his chariot.'

Zeal is a passion, drive, inner desire, and an enthusiastic diligence. It produces an initiative and eagerness to pursue an inner desire with determination and perseverance. Passion stirs you up to release an inner endowment. Zeal is located in the heart of a person. The heart of a man is the spirit of a man.

Exodus 35:30-33 (New King James Version)
'And Moses said to the children of Israel, "See, the LORD has called by name Bezalel the son of Uri, the son of Hur, of the tribe of Judah; and He has filled him with the Spirit of God, in wisdom and understanding, in knowledge and all manner of workmanship, to design artistic works, to work in gold and silver and bronze, in cutting jewels for setting, in carving wood, and to work in all manner of artistic workmanship.'

When the Holy Spirit inhabits your spirit, which is your heart, the wisdom, understanding, knowledge, all manners of skills and designs to fulfil divine purpose will be imparted into you. The ability, divine enablement, or anointing to fulfil purpose will drive you into your destiny route. This enthusiastic drive is a deposition of a strong urge in a heart towards a particular skill or gifting. The passion will stir up the skill in you for the purpose of fulfilment.

Passion reveals purpose. It puts a round peg in a round hole. Where there is passion, there is the ability to perform excellently. Where there is passion, there is God's Spirit to grant innovations.

Refiner's fire: in geology, an ore is defined as a mineral that contains a commercially useful material, such as gold or uranium. It is a naturally occurring mineral or rock from which a valuable or useful substance, especially a metal, can be extracted at a reasonable cost.

Ore deposits are mined and processed to recover a metal or applicable substance. The process of recovery is called refining. The refinery uses fire that produces intense heat at very high temperatures. This intense heat removes impurities. Impurities are unwanted substances that reduce the value of the metal. In the course of burning or heating the ore, its real value is revealed.

Destinies and divine purposes can be revealed by fire. Sometimes, God allows a man to go through fire in order for him to find purpose. No one likes the fire, although, it is one of the channels of purification. When you're purified, your true value becomes exposed and noticed.

Malachi 3:3 (New King James Version)
'He will sit as a refiner and a purifier of silver; He will purify the sons of Levi, and purge them as gold and silver, that they may offer to the LORD an offering in righteousness.'

An offering in righteousness is divine purpose, and can only be presented to God in purity. To purify this offering, it must go through the refiner's fire; otherwise, it won't be acceptable. The purging of gold and silver is not an enjoyable process. When you go through fire, you either burn or refine, it depends on your material content. Woods become charcoal and ashes; silver and gold become treasures. The fire burns out the wood

101

in you, but brings out the purpose that is hidden within you. Your divine purpose is gold. If you find it, you find treasure. Your divine purpose is silver, when you locate it, you locate wealth.

If you're going through fire that is God-made, it is for your good. After the flame, you will come out a better person. When you come out, you won't only have treasures, you will become a treasure. A man with divine purpose is a treasure to his generation and after. Treasures boost economic growths in any society. Treasures add value to nations. We are all in a raw state, until we yield ourselves to the refinery to expose our real reasons for existence.

Dreams and visions: some years ago, as I woke up one morning to have my devotion, I had an unusual spiritual experience. Within seconds after kneeling beside my bed to pray, I fell into a trance. In that vision, an angel of the Lord brought a book, and dropped it beside me. I saw the back cover of the book, with a pencil-shaded colour. I also saw that there were two authors; me and another person that I'm not ready to describe. I can still recall the face of that person and what he was wearing. This happened more than twenty years ago. To date, I haven't met the person. The vision gave me a vivid picture of my divine calling in the area of writing.

In those days, I was just involved in writing undocumented poems, and later did a bit of song writing. I wrote more than 200 songs and poems, and even went to the studio to record a demo. Despite all these, I still didn't feel that inner satisfaction. I broke my demo cassette, and threw it in the bin. I also threw away my poetry books. In 2006, while sitting on bus number 38, from Lower Clapton to Dalston in London, the Lord started ministering to me. He reminded me of the vision I had about twenty years back. He told me that my success in life is tied to me obeying my heavenly call. He made it clear that if I don't obey, I will keep struggling in life. I struggled for four more years before I finally followed His instruction. One day, I was fed up of living in a circle, so I decided to do a nine hour non-stop intercessory prayer. All through the prayer, I only spoke in the Tongue of the Holy Spirit. A week after the prayer, one evening as I came back from the service, my wife began to appeal to me to start writing. I gave her reasons why I can't. Late that night, the Lord again started prompting me. He told me to listen to her. That was the last word that spurred me into action. Within four months, I wrote two books. 'Finding Real Purpose' is one of the products of those four months.

Genesis 37:9 (New King James Version)
'Then he dreamed still another dream and told it to his brothers, and said, "Look, I have dreamed another dream. And this time, the sun, the moon, and the eleven stars bowed down to me."'

God reveals divine purposes through dreams and visions. It doesn't matter if it is an open or closed vision, just be sensitive. Vision identifies future positioning, and exposes it to the visionary. God uses dreams and visions to inform and direct a person about his destination in life. In my pains, my visions have always been my gain. When God shows you your end, the journey becomes more bearable. If you must find purpose in life, you must dream again and again, whether people like it or not. Your folks may not like it. Your parents may be against it, just keep dreaming.

WALKING IN DIVINE PURPOSE

There is a difference between knowing something and experiencing what you know. If you discover divine purpose and do not step into it, you cannot walk in it. Discovery comes from exploration and seeking, while walking in discovery is the main work. We should realise that an open door is different from walking into a house. When a door opens, it is the responsibility of the person standing outside to take advantage of it. Doors don't stay open for too long, otherwise, they will attract unwanted guests. When your door opens, step in. Discovery is an open door for all-round promotion, economic growth, and inner fulfilment. If you walk in it, you will thrive in it.

To help you walk in divine purpose, you need to;

Be a mentee: a mentee is a person who is guided by a mentor. A mentor is a wise and trusted counsellor, adviser, or teacher. He is an influential senior sponsor or supporter. The synonyms of a mentor are teacher, guide, coach, tutor, preceptor, and master.

There is nothing new on earth. There is no position or height you want to reach that no one has never reached or even exceeded. There are lots of people on earth already operating in your expected goals and desire. You won't be the first to dream it, or get there. There are those whom God has given the keys to your dreams and aspirations in life. When you discover these people and submit yourself to them, the journey becomes easier for you. Your submission will help you avoid the same errors they made on their way up. Being under a mentor speeds up the fulfilment of divine purpose. If you want to become a lone ranger, your destination may be out of reach.

Romans 13:1-3 (New King James Version)
'Let every soul be subject to the governing authorities. For there is no authority except from God, and the authorities that exist are appointed by God. Therefore whoever resists the authority resists the ordinance of God, and those who resist will bring judgment on themselves. For rulers are not a terror to good works, but to evil. Do you want to be unafraid of the authority? Do what is good, and you will have praise from the same.'

Those who refuse mentoring have mental problems. Pride and arrogance are insanities that destroy destinies. If you're not subject to anyone, life will subject you. If there is no one on earth you can learn from, soon, people will begin to learn from your errors. Some people's destinies have been crippled because they just can't see the danger of not understudying successful people. If you study success, you will avoid failure. If you learn from authority, you will avoid being at the bottom. I cannot teach you if you cannot subject yourself. You cannot learn with your wings spread out. Except the lady stoops, she cannot conquer. If you refuse to recognise a governing authority, you are not recognising God. If you can't learn from leadership, you will always be led. Great minds learn from great people. Successful attitude imbibes the culture of successful people. The best way up is down. If you refuse to kneel, you can't reach heaven.

A mentee is submissive, humble, teachable, patient, observant, and proactive. The level of anointing that accompanies your divine purpose is a function of your level of submission. Jesus mentored about 70 disciples, only 11 came out successful. Out of the 11, just four of them really made a great impact.

Moses was mentored by his father-in-law; Jethro. Jethro taught him policies, administration and government. If Moses had carried on with the style of government he learned whilst in Egypt, he would have died early. The Egyptian system of government would have destroyed the children of Israel in the wilderness. The governmental system in Egypt was too autocratic and too monologues. It was a system where the king judged every case. Egypt's governmental system was too centralised. Jethro taught Moses how to decentralise government. He taught him how to put government more in the hands of the people. As a result, they had something similar to legislators, governors, and counsellors.

Exodus 18:17-23 (New King James Version)
'So Moses' father-in-law said to him, "The thing that you do is not good. Both you and these people who are with you will surely wear yourselves out. For this thing is too much for you; you are not able to perform it by yourself. Listen now to my voice; I will give you counsel, and God will be with you: Stand before God for the people, so that you may bring the difficulties to God. And you shall teach them the statutes and the laws, and show them the way in which they must walk and the work they must do. Moreover you shall select from all the people able men, such as fear God, men of truth, hating covetousness; and place such over them to be rulers of thousands, rulers of hundreds, rulers of fifties, and rulers of tens. And let them judge the people at all times. Then it will be that every great matter they shall bring to you, but every small matter they themselves shall judge. So it will be easier for you, for they will bear the burden with you. If you do this thing, and God so commands you, then you will be able to endure, and all this people will also go to their place in peace."

Little Samuel learned from Eli. He learned how to hear and respond to the voice of God. Elisha learned from Elijah and he received a double portion of his anointing. Nehemiah was a cup-bearer to King Artaxerxes; he rebuilt the wall of Jerusalem. Mordecai was a gatekeeper to King Ahasuerus; he delivered Israel from destruction. Timothy was mentored by Apostle Paul; he fulfilled the work of the ministry.

Purpose enjoys serving. As you serve, understudy who you're serving. It is wrong to serve ignorantly. Servers must be observers. When you serve, observe methodologies, character, decision making processes, speeches, likes and dislikes, organisational styles, perceptions, accountability, value systems, actions and reactions, etc.

My best method of studying mentors is from a distance. I'm not a question asking type of person. I prefer to look into what you do, how you do it, who you do it with, when you do it, the words of your mouth and the corresponding actions, how you carry yourself, etc. If you tell one story twice, I compare the two illustrations to see if there are variations. The presence or absence of variations gives me an idea of who you are. I am able to predict almost 70 percent of what a person is thinking from their body language. You can be mentored without the knowledge of the mentor.

Be prepared: preparation involves studying, planning, and setting targets to achieve your purpose. A call to divine purpose is not a call to mediocrity. Purpose is far more difficult than proposition. To get the best of destiny, you must study its contents. Having a shallow knowledge of your calling can only lead to being lukewarm. To go far, you must go deep. Depth and height are related.

Hosea 4:6 (New King James Version)
'My people are destroyed for lack of knowledge. Because you have rejected knowledge, I also will reject you from being priest for Me; because you have forgotten the law of your God, I also will forget your children.'

Lack of information is destructive. Information reforms; ignorance deforms. In divine calling, you must know the truth and the fact. You must also know the difference between truth and fact. You must be wise to understand when a fact is very useful, and its application. The truth sets you free, but the fact helps you make good use of your freedom. If you know the truth but don't know the fact, the children of this world will bamboozle you. Secular education is very necessary in producing the fact. Mentally lazy Christians eschew the fact and only hold on to the truth. To reign in life and conquer territories, a combination of truth and fact is very vital. Information technology is a fact, how good are you in it?

If you don't study your calling, you will be rejected. If you don't regularly update yourself in your divine purpose, you will soon quickly run out of steam. If you run out of fuel, you become immobile. Immobility cannot take you to your destiny. Remember, destiny is destination.

Psalm 42:7 (New King James Version)
'Deep calls unto deep at the noise of Your waterfalls; all Your waves and billows have gone over me.'

The strong currents of waterfalls are used to generate hydroelectricity. Angel falls in Venezuela is the world's tallest waterfall. It is about 3212 feet or 979 metres tall. The depth of Angel falls is intimidating. In the same vein, the depth of knowledge intimidates ignorance. When you possess an in-depth understanding of your calling and every other necessary information useful in life, the wave you produce will generate energy. This energy will become the capacity of a system to do work. The work done by a deep understanding speaks for itself. Purpose fulfilled with deep revealed knowledge is eternal.

In planning, you must take into consideration time management, the use of professionals where necessary, people management, cost management, marketing management, accounts management, etc. You must also set measurable and realistic goals.

Luke 14:28-30 (New King James Version)
'For which of you, intending to build a tower, does not sit down first and count the cost, whether he has enough to finish it — lest, after he has laid the foundation, and is not able to finish, all who see it begin to mock him, saying, "This man began to build and was not able to finish"?'

To *'sit down first and count the cost'* is planning. Accountability is planning. If you cannot count, you will be shamed. You must count the cost of every relevant resource you require to fulfil your purpose in life. Counting is not a one off event, it is instantaneous and continuous. You can only count when you sit down first. You don't plan on the street or whilst in a queue. You plan sitting down. Planning must not be done under pressure or stress. Planning is not done on the move. A life time expectation is not written on pieces of paper. Planners are builders. They achieve their life expectations because they respect the principles of planning. Children's educations are not planned in the car. How can you plan a destiny in a depreciating asset?

Be sensitive to timing: any purpose that has no timing is a waste of time.

Ecclesiastes 3:1 (New King James Version)
'To everything there is a season, a time for every purpose under heaven.'

Divine purpose has a maturity stage. A man can abort his destiny with haste, or delay it with procrastination or insensitivity. You must be sensitive to the time of your purpose. This sensitivity comes from your inner man.

1 chronicles 12:32 (New King James Version)
'Of the sons of Issachar who had understanding of the times, to know what Israel ought to do, their chiefs were two hundred; and all their brethren were at their command;'

To fulfil divine purpose, you must have an understanding of the times, to know what you ought to do. When the Spirit bids you go, go, but if not, wait. There is always a time for everyone who waits on God. Those who wait until it is their time don't struggle.

Make a move: learning, preparation, planning, and sensitivity become impotent if no action is taken. Faith without a corresponding action is dead. You can only step into purpose and walk in it by faith. As you walk, resources for manifestation become available. If you hang on to a place of no destiny, you become an object of ridicule devoid of peace and joy. Hanging on to such places can hang a person.

Deuteronomy 1:6-8 (New King James Version)
'The LORD our God spoke to us in Horeb, saying: "You have dwelt long enough at this mountain. Turn and take your journey, and go to the mountains of the Amorites, to all the neighboring places in the plain, in the mountains and in the lowland, in the South and on the seacoast, to the land of the Canaanites and to Lebanon, as far as the great river, the River Euphrates. See, I have set the land before you; go in and possess the land which the LORD swore to your fathers—to Abraham, Isaac, and Jacob—to give to them and their descendants after them.'

Comfort zones eat up divine destinations. Mount Horeb is a symbol of a good position but not a good destination. Your divine purpose is far greater than your comfort. Your destiny is your promise land. Your divine purpose takes you back to the Garden of Eden. You must be bold to go. You need to show strength, agility, and the willingness to start moving. Your destiny is achievable because Divinity has given it to you. You can make it if you move. Take the first step and start something.

Understand that your beginning will be small: when the earth was without form and void and God said 'Let there be light', people with no vision and faith would have said, 'What

111

is the essence of light in a shapeless world? Of what significance is it?' With God, every beginning starts as a seed. Light is a seed. Every embryo starts as a cell. The beginning of a future is a cell. Any vision that does not have a small beginning is a magical one. Magic is temporal, fake, over-estimated, and empty. If you don't have the character of growing from small to big, you're in danger. When you look into the antecedent of any one that God has used, whether in Bible days or our present world, they all started small. It is only fools that start big and end being small. Big fools start very big and end up very small. Not that they were actually big to begin with, they were only big in their own vague imaginations.

Job 8:7 (New King James Version)
'Though your beginning was small, yet your latter end would increase abundantly.'

A small start does not necessarily mean a small end. An invested purpose increases abundantly at the latter end. The latter end is the day of harvest. It is the pay day and the hour of accountability. Beginnings are always small, ends aren't. To those who invest in their purpose, there is a continual bumper harvest. But for others who did otherwise, the end is either small or has nothing to show for it.

The fact that a beginning is small is not a statement of probability but truth. Understanding this truth puts a person in a position of humility to cultivate the farm of purpose by applying the character of due diligence.

Zechariah 4:10 (New King James Version)
'For who has despised the day of small things? For these seven rejoice to see the plumb line in the hand of Zerubbabel. They are the eyes of the LORD, which scan to and fro throughout the whole earth.'

You should never despise the plumb line on your hand. A plumb line is a cord or string from which a metal weight is suspended pointing directly to the earth's centre of gravity, used to determine the vertical from a given point. If you search for the picture of a plumb line on the internet, you will be surprised how thin and fragile it looks. In spite of its smallness, it carries a metal plumb bob that determines vertical positions. If the seven rejoice seeing the plumb line on your hand, why are you despising it? If God is excited about your vision, why are you calling it small?

Your beginning will not be perfect: no beginning is ever perfect. Growth is an upward movement from imperfection to perfection. When God created the world, it was not excellent but good. When a thing is good, there is room for improvement. If your beginning is perfect, there will be nothing to work on.

Psalm 139:16 (The Message)
'Like an open book, you watched me grow from conception to birth; all the stages of my life were spread out before you, the days of my life all prepared before I'd even lived one day.'

In purpose fulfilment, there are growth stages from conception to birth. Even after birth, there are more stages before you get to your destination. There is no abracadabra in the fulfilment of a person's destiny. Don't be discouraged by an imperfect start. Just keep doing the right things and the right results will start coming in.

Close your mind to fame: fame is different from recognition. Fame gives you celebrity status; recognition puts you on the spot where your giftings can be seen. You need recognition to promote your talent, calling and ministry. The truth is that you don't need fame. Fame is a distraction; recognition is a light. Recognition makes people acknowledge, appreciate, and realise you. A city on a hill is recognised. A lamp on a lamp stand gives light. It will amount to hypocrisy to say that you don't want to be recognised. If you're not recognised, no one can benefit from your gift. If no one benefits from you, you won't benefit from anyone. Every gifted person needs a platform of recognition in order to breakthrough. Fame kills; recognition encourages.

113

Matthew 6:1-2 (New King James Version)
'Take heed that you do not do your charitable deeds before men, to be seen by them. Otherwise you have no reward from your Father in heaven. Therefore, when you do a charitable deed, do not sound a trumpet before you as the hypocrites do in the synagogues and in the streets, that they may have glory from men. Assuredly, I say to you, they have their reward.'

Fame is noisy. Fame advertises its charitable work before men in the market place in order to receive the praises of men. Today's market place is the media. Fame is hypocritical. An example of recognition is seen in the following passage:

Matthew 5:16 (New King James Version)
'Let your light so shine before men, that they may see your good works and glorify your Father in heaven.'

Matthew 7:24–25 (New King James Version)
'Therefore whoever hears these sayings of Mine, and does them, I will liken him to a wise man who built his house on the rock: and the rain descended, the floods came, and the winds blew and beat on that house; and it did not fall, for it was founded on the rock.'

It is not easy to climb a hill. It takes a lot of strength and energy to get to the top of it. Building a house on a hill is very laborious, let alone, building a city. Imagine yourself being involved in carrying all the materials needed for the construction of a city to a hill. Imagine carrying all the metals, pillars, cements, bricks etc, to a hill, then you will understand better what it takes. Anyone who builds on a hill deserves acknowledgement, appreciation, and realisation.

A lot goes into laying a foundation on a rock. In those days, there weren't high-tech equipment used to break rocks. Builders used hammers to crack rocks with their hands. Until dynamite was discovered, this was the practice. To dig a foundation for a building on a rock with bare hands is very tasking. Anyone who does not recognise the person who lays a foundation on a rock is not being nice.

In pursuing divine purpose, never seek fame. Be a builder. Don't build on sand but on hills and rocks.

Be ready for enemies: life has structured itself in such a way that not everyone will like your dreams, visions, aspirations, or drive. The enemies of visions are of two types; the friendly and unfriendly. The friendly mean no harm, but are very harmful. Some friendly enemies discourage you by telling you how high the mountain is, and how impossible it is to climb. Other friendly enemies engage you in time wasting activities that make you lose focus. The unfriendly enemies engage you in a head-on collision. They are hostile and ready to sell you like a slave so that your dreams never come to fruition. So, life produces side attractions and side distractions, but whatever action it is, the sole reason is to devour your destiny. The subtle aspect of enemies is that they want you to make your vision a part-time job and your distractions a full time job.

When you dream big dreams, you incur the wrath of household enemies. Household enemies are enemies within your family. Joseph's brothers hated him, not because of his coat of many colours, but because of his dreams. When people can't comprehend your divine purpose, they get angry. People, who are going nowhere, hate those who are going somewhere. They prefer it, when everyone remains stagnant. People with no divine intention want everyone to be purposeless. They understand that people of purpose are people of promotion. Since they don't want you to leave them at the lower cadre, they manipulate you to stay down.

Matthew 13:53-57 (The Message Bible Version)
When Jesus finished telling these stories, he left there, returned to his hometown, and gave a lecture in the meetinghouse. He made a real hit, impressing everyone. "We had no idea he was this good!" they said. "How did he get so wise, get such ability?" But in the next breath they were cutting him down: "We've known him since he was a kid; he's the carpenter's son. We know his mother, Mary. We know his brothers James and Joseph, Simon and Judas. All his sisters live here. Who does he think he is?"

They got their noses all out of joint.

Beware of homeboys especially in a hometown. Familiarity actually breeds contempt. There is no relationship between being impressed and accepting a message. Some people, who scream most during a sermon, may not necessarily be doers of the word, while others, who keep calm, may just be assessing your level of intelligence and grading you. The people you impress may in the next second be the ones to cut you down. Those who know your history are the first set of people to disbelieve you. Charity may begin at home, but marketing your giftings does not. Before returning home, sell yourself outside. If your market place is in the home, you won't go far. In destiny fulfilment, working from home is not advisable. When your vision grows, go out of home. Remaining at home confines your dream to the size of your home. If the rain, sun, snow, and wind do not descend on you, your vision is small. Home is an enemy to big dreams. If your vision has grown to the stage of renting a place, go out and pay the rent. If you don't challenge yourself, you will remain in a comfort zone. Home is too comfortable for divine purpose.

Be aware of God's helpers: when you're truly in your God-given purpose, He will send helpers to assist you. God never allows purpose-driven people to walk alone. He sends men, women, and angels to assist them. From all spheres of life, God will bring people to help you shoulder part of the responsibilities. Be aware that God sends people when the load is too heavy for you. If you can carry the load, asking for helpers is a sign of laziness. If you need helpers, expand your vision.

All big visionaries need helpers. To finish well, you need the right people and resources. You can't achieve big dreams alone.

Exodus 18:21-23 (new King James version)
'Moreover you shall select from all the people able men, such as fear God, men of truth, hating covetousness; and place such over them to be rulers of thousands, rulers of hundreds, rulers of fifties, and rulers of tens. And let them judge the people at all times. Then it will be that every great matter they shall bring to you, but every small matter they themselves shall judge. So it will be easier for you, for they will bear the burden with you. If you do this thing, and God so commands you, then you will be able to endure, and all this people will also go to their place in peace.'

Government and administration are the keys to managing divine purpose. It takes the right people to make up a good government. Where there is delegation of duties and a good judicial system, purpose can never fail. When God brings helpers your way, your ability to form a defined structure will produce order. Structure must always guide your methods of operation. Where there is no structure, there is no discipline. Indiscipline punctuates destiny.

Never give up: Robert Schuller, in one of his books titled *'Tough times never last but tough people do'* says, *'When the going gets tough, the tough gets going'*. It is tough people that embark on divine purpose not weaklings. It is far more preferable to go through the pains of purpose than swim in the pond of stagnancy. Instead of breaking into a new realm, some people are paddling in the pond of comfort. Those on a mission don't look back. You must make your vision a mission if you have been commissioned.

Luke 9:62 (New King James Version)
'But Jesus said to him, "No one, having put his hand to the plow, and looking back, is fit for the kingdom of God."'

You can't afford to look back. There is danger in looking back.

117

When you put your hand on the plough and look back, you will miss your target. Looking back turns you into a pillar of salt, then, you get easily washed away by the rain. If you don't want to drip down the valley in the form of dissolved salt, never give up. Never give up your dream, vision, and divine purpose. Yes, it is tough, but you're tougher. It is rough, but you're rugged. You can achieve it, make it, and get there!

THE SIGNIFICANCE AND BENEFITS OF DIVINE PURPOSE

Divine purpose does not have demerits or disadvantages. It is significant, beneficial, productive, and lucrative. Divine purpose is all-round fulfilling.

Some of the significance and benefits of divine purpose are:

Divine purpose produces inward satisfaction: until you're where God wants you to be, you can't have the satisfaction that your soul longs for. You may have money and other material wealth, yet be devoid of fulfilment.

Psalm 40:6-8 (New King James Version)
'Sacrifice and offering You did not desire; My ears You have opened. Burnt offering and sin offering You did not require. Then I said, "Behold, I come; in the scroll of the book it is written of me. I delight to do Your will, O my God, and Your law is within my heart."'

A delight is a high degree of pleasure or enjoyment, joy, rapture, and satisfaction. When your delight is in God's divine intention, you will have inward satisfaction. Divine purpose fills the vacuum that sacrifice and offering cannot.

Divine purpose produces inward peace: peace stills inward violence. The best way to kill worries is to live in your purpose. Anxieties submit to a purposeful life. When you walk in your calling, you take the pressures of this life off your shoulders, and the yoke of struggling off your neck. The anointing that fulfils divine destiny is a yoke destroyer.

Psalm 4:7-8 (New King James Version)
'You have put gladness in my heart, more than in the season that their grain and wine increased. I will both lie down in peace, and sleep; for You alone, O LORD, make me dwell in safety.'

Peace in the storm, and joy in the heart, is what God gives to those who do His will. You cannot walk in divine purpose and be restless. Peace and joy locate heavenly callings.

Divine purpose boosts confidence: confidence is an assurance that makes you know who you are, what you are, where you are, and where you're going. Confidence gives you full trust, belief, and reliability. When you're confident, you're determined, resolute, and pragmatic in your certainty.

Philippians 1:6 (New King James Version)
'Being confident of this very thing, that He who has begun a good work in you will complete it until the day of Jesus Christ;'

Confidence gives you an assurance of completion. It makes you realise that you're neither the beginner nor the end of the good work of purpose, so, you don't need to worry. This understanding takes a lot of pressure off you. What God has started, He will finish. You're only a conduit not the Conductor. You're the pipeline, He is the Engineer.

Divine purpose reassures: a reassurance is a repeated assurance or confidence. There is a stage you get to in the affairs of life and ministry that you need a double assurance. When the forces of discouragement come like a flood and the tidal waves of the storm hit violently on the boat taking you to your destination, double confidence becomes expedient.

Matthew 11:2-6 (New King James Version)
'And when John had heard in prison about the works of Christ, he sent two of his disciples and said to Him, "Are You the Coming One, or do we look for another?" Jesus answered and said to them, "Go and tell John the things which you hear and see: The blind see and the lame walk; the lepers are cleansed and the deaf hear; the dead are raised up and the poor have the gospel preached to them. And blessed is he who is not offended because of Me."'

In prison, John the Baptist was reassured. When divine purpose is re-echoed, mental noise and confusion become silent. Reassurance erases irritation in times of palpitation. There are times in your calling when your heartbeat becomes rapid. Going back to re-read the vision calms the boiling nerves and keeps you going.

Divine purpose coordinates diversification: the power to coordinate is in divine purpose. Visions do multiply but coordination unifies them.

Romans 8:28 (New King James Version)
'And we know that all things work together for good to those who love God, to those who are the called according to His purpose.'

Togetherness is a unification of ideas that form a coordinate force to achieve unimaginable results. It merges result oriented goals, and directs them towards a specific target that pleases God. Purpose is a coordinator.

Divine purpose attracts divine recognition: heaven knows it's own. On the last day, those who walked in real purpose will see God. Those who didn't will also see Him, but hear something different from those who did. There is a big difference between the two sets of seers.

Matthew 25:34-36 (New King James Version)
'Then the King will say to those on His right hand, 'Come, you blessed of My Father, inherit the kingdom prepared for you from the

foundation of the world: for I was hungry and you gave Me food; I was thirsty and you gave Me drink; I was a stranger and you took Me in; I was naked and you clothed Me; I was sick and you visited Me; I was in prison and you came to Me."'

There is right hand recognition for those who walk according to God's purpose on earth. God knows them by their names, and answers them speedily. If heaven does not recognise you, you may have strayed out of purpose, or maybe, you were never there.

Recognition brings acceptance. It boosts your ego and confidence. It takes away fear and makes you enjoy the redemptive work.

Where there is divine purpose there is divine blessing: blessing is all encompassing, total, and wholesome. It goes beyond any dictionary definition. Any good thing that God does not withhold from His own is a blessing.

Psalm 84:11 (New King James Version)
'For the LORD God is a sun and shield; the LORD will give grace and glory; no good thing will He withhold from those who walk uprightly.'

Walking uprightly is walking in divine purpose. In your purpose, the Lord will be your sun and shield. The sun will energise you, while the shield will defend you. Grace and glory will be made available for you.

Ephesians 1:3 (New King James Version)
'Blessed be the God and Father of our Lord Jesus Christ, who has blessed us with every spiritual blessing in the heavenly places in Christ.'

When you walk with God, you will have access to every spiritual blessing in the heavenly places in Christ. The word, *'every'* means there is no limitation. Every blessing is all blessings not most blessings. Heaven has places, and for each place, there is a special blessing. You are bound by heavenly mandate to have access to all the regions. If you access the health region, you will live in divine health. If you access the region of prosperity, you are bound to prosper. Where you access is what you receive. If you use your key to access all regions, you will live an unlimited life.

Divine purpose promulgates a generational inheritance: when you walk in purpose, the benefits don't end with you. Purpose produces a cascade of blessings from generation to generation.

Genesis 17:7 (New King James Version)
'And I will establish My covenant between Me and you and your descendants after you in their generations, for an everlasting covenant, to be God to you and your descendants after you.'

When God gives a vision, it doesn't end with the visionary. Divine purpose is never selfish but goes from generation to generation. A vision plan must be older than the visionary's life expectancy. Policy designs must exceed the designer's retirement age. It is a failure for a visionary not to leave a success plan before exiting the stage. Elijah left a success plan; his mantle. Elisha left a success plan; his bones. Jesus left a success plan; the Holy Spirit.

Divine purpose builds divine protection: you can't walk with God and be vulnerable. You can't be in divine purpose and be unprotected. Purpose strengthens your defence.

Job 1:10 (New King James Version)
'Have You not made a hedge around him, around his household, and around all that he has on every side? You have blessed the work of his hands, and his possessions have increased in the land.'

A hedge is a boundary or barrier surrounding a thing or person with the intention to protect, restrict, and obstruct invaders. Protection is a method of preservation.

When you walk in your calling, God builds a hedge around you, your family, and all that is connected to you. The hedge cannot be gate-crashed by enemies, no matter how intelligent their devices are.

2 Samuel 22:1 (New King James Version)
'Then David spoke to the LORD the words of this song, on the day when the LORD had delivered him from the hand of all his enemies, and from the hand of Saul.'

When you walk in divine purpose, you will be delivered from all your enemies. If you walk out of purpose, you will be exposed to danger. God is a Rock, Fortress, Deliverer, Strength, Shield, Horn of salvation, Stronghold, and Refuge to those who are the called according to His purpose.

Divine purpose makes room and attracts divine provision: where there is purpose, there is provision. Answered prayer locates planned purposes. The more you dig into your purpose, the more you increase the room for provision. The size of your provision is the size of your purpose.

Psalm 92:12-15 (New King James Version)
'The righteous shall flourish like a palm tree, he shall grow like a cedar in Lebanon. Those who are planted in the house of the LORD shall flourish in the courts of our God. They shall still bear fruit in old age; they shall be fresh and flourishing, to declare that the LORD is upright; He is my rock, and there is no unrighteousness in Him.'

Bearing fruit in old age is making profits in old age. Even at retirement, those who have sown will continue to reap. People who walk in divine purpose don't depend on pensions or government benefits. In old age, they are still fruitful, growing, fresh and flourishing.

Divine purpose earns you respect: respect grants you consideration, appreciation, connection, recognition, and a testimony. Respect is an esteem for or a sense of the worth or excellence of a person, personal quality or ability. It is something considered as a manifestation of a personal quality or ability.

Joshua 3:7 (New King James Version)
'And the LORD said to Joshua, "This day I will begin to exalt you in the sight of all Israel, that they may know that, as I was with Moses, so I will be with you.'

Respect exalts you before the led. If you're not respected by subordinates, your leadership will be in doubt. When you're diligent in your calling, God will exalt you before the people. Your level of respect for God determines the level of people's respect for you. When God makes you big in the sight of people, they will follow your instructions.

Divine purpose makes you stand with kings: purpose associates you with royalty. If you excel in your calling, you will wine and dine with the best.

Proverbs 22:29 (New King James Version)
'Do you see a man who excels in his work? He will stand before kings; he will not stand before unknown men.'

A man who excels in divine purpose is a king in what he does. Kings stand with kings. Mere men stand with mere men. Until you embrace purpose, you will keep kneeling before kings. Those who are in their destinies stand with people of destiny. Those who are out of purpose bow to those in purpose. You invite an insult to yourself if you do not know your destination. No one in the street has the time to describe a direction for someone who does not know his destination. If you keep guessing in life, life will keep you guessing.

A deep sea does not call a stream. If you want to be called by the deep, you must also be deep. The people who dig deep meet treasures. The shallow minded opt for shallow ideas and stampede into shallow results. No one can stampede into royalty, it comes by birth. This birth is a product of the travail of diligence. Diligence is purified by pains and endurance. It comes out better from a furnace of fire.

Divine purpose grows divine relationship: walking in divine purpose increases your affinity with God and good people. Divine purpose does not pitch you against destiny fulfillers. If you're always at rivalry with purposeful people, there must be something wrong.

James 2:23-24 (New King James Version)
'And the Scripture was fulfilled which says, "Abraham believed God, and it was accounted to him for righteousness." And he was called the friend of God. You see then that a man is justified by works, and not by faith only.'

When your work is justified, your divine relationship is solidified. The extent of your relationship with God is proof of the extent at which you're ready to go with your divine purpose.

Divine purpose births stars: according to NASA, a star is a huge shining ball in space that produces a tremendous amount of light and other forms of energy. The sun is an example of a star.

There are different types of stars which also come in different sizes. The sun is one of the smallest stars. It is considered by astronomers as a dwarf because there are supergiant stars that are about one thousand times bigger than the sun. The smallest stars known as neutrons have a radius of about 6 miles or 10 kilometres.

The characteristics of stars include; brightness, surface temperature, colour, size, and mass. The coolest stars have a surface temperature of about 3,000 degrees centigrade, while the hottest soar above 5,000 degrees centigrade. Stars are massive, very voluminous, emit great intensity of light, produce great amounts of heat energy, etc. As a result of their energy emission, they support life on earth. They are the source of food production through the process of photosynthesis, technological inventions, and developmental research.

God is very passionate about stars. He uses them to symbolise greatness and multiplication.

Genesis 22:17 (New King James Version)
'Blessing I will bless you, and multiplying I will multiply your descendants as the stars of the heaven and as the sand which is on the seashore; and your descendants shall possess the gate of their enemies.'

When you function in your purpose, you are a star, and stars do multiply. Being a star means, you will emit light and heat at unbelievable intensities; you will shine, support the existence of life, become colourful, have great volume, and become massive.

Job 22:12 (New King James Version)
'Is not God in the height of heaven? And see the highest stars, how lofty they are!'

Stars occupy the highest heights in the heavenlies. The sun is the closest star to the earth, and has a light year of 0.000016. Light years are used to measure the distance of the star to the earth. It is defined as the distance that light travels to the earth in a year. The distance of the sun to the earth therefore, is 0.000016 multiplied by 9463700000000 kilometres. Some stars like sigma 2398 have 11.6 as a light year. So, its distance to earth is 11.6 multiplied by that huge number.

Walking in divine purpose puts you in the highest position. You're compared to a star when you follow God's design for your life.

Psalm 136:7-9 (New King James Version)
'To Him who made great lights, for His mercy endures forever — The sun to rule by day, for His mercy endures forever; the moon and stars to rule by night, for His mercy endures forever.'

Stars rule by day and night. Walking in divine purpose gives you leadership ability. In purpose, you are endowed with the power to control, direct, and exercise authority.

Daniel 12:3 (New King James Version)
'Those who are wise shall shine like the brightness of the firmament, and those who turn many to righteousness like the stars forever and ever.'

Wise people stick to divine calling. As a result, they are like ageless stars. Purposeful people don't die; they live on forever and ever.

1 Corinthians 15:41 (New King James Version)
'There is one glory of the sun, another glory of the moon, and another glory of the stars; for one star differs from another star in glory.'

Stars are glorious. Divine purpose is glorious. People who pursue destiny are like glorious stars.

Genesis 37:9 (New King James Version)
'Then he dreamed still another dream and told it to his brothers, and said, "Look, I have dreamed another dream. And this time, the sun, the moon, and the eleven stars bowed down to me."'

Stars respect divine positions. They bow down to higher callings. They're never envious, neither do they hate dreamers. Stars are never arrogant.

Job 38:7 (New King James Version)
'When the morning stars sang together, and all the sons of God shouted for joy?'

Psalm 148:3 (New King James Version)
'Praise Him, sun and moon; Praise Him, all you stars of light!'

Stars sing and praise God. Divine purpose is a praise singer. Divine purpose shouts for joy. If there is no song of praise in your purpose, it is not divine.

Stars fight against destiny quenchers. They fight for carriers of divine purpose. They are not cowards, neither are they intimidated by enemies.

Judges 5:20 (New King James Version)
'They fought from the heavens; the stars from their courses fought against Sisera.'

Sisera was the captain of the army of Jabin, King of Canaan. He had 900 iron chariots, and oppressed Israel for 20 years. He had a fortified Calvary base called Harosheth Haggoyim. Sisera existed in the days of Deborah.

According to Midrash, Sisera hitherto had conquered every country against which he had fought. His voice was so strong that when he called loudly, the most solid wall would shake, and the wildest animals would fall dead. Deborah was the only one who could withstand his voice and remain unshaken.

God used Barak and a troop of ten thousand men from Naphtali and Zebulun to defeat Sisera and his army. He was later killed by a woman called Jael.

If your star doesn't fight from God's course, you cannot defeat a Sisera. Stars don't get intimidated by bullies. Divine purpose can never be bullied to submission. You can't surrender your divine mandate because you feel someone doesn't like it. You must fight, not just for your course but from your course.

Stars inform, guide, and direct.

Matthew 2:2, 9 and 10 (New King James Version)
'Saying, "Where is He who has been born King of the Jews? For we have seen His star in the East and have come to worship Him."

When they heard the king, they departed; and behold, the star which they had seen in the East went before them, till it came and stood over where the young Child was. When they saw the star, they rejoiced with exceedingly great joy.'

Stars inform, guide, and direct you to the King of kings, the salvation Giver, and destiny Fulfiller. Stars don't settle at the palace of earthly royalty, they move on to heavenly destiny. Stars tell you the right place to enter and who to bow to. Their guidance and direction bring you exceeding great joy. Divine purpose births stars!

Divine purpose keeps you in covenant: the best way to remain in God's covenant is to walk in His purpose. A derailed purpose is a derailed covenant. You can't be out of purpose and assume that you will keep enjoying covenant benefits. It doesn't work that way.

Leviticus 26:14-16 (New King James Version)
'But if you do not obey Me, and do not observe all these commandments, and if you despise My statutes, or if your soul abhors My judgments, so that you do not perform all My commandments, but break My covenant, I also will do this to you: I will even appoint terror over you, wasting disease and fever which shall consume the eyes and cause sorrow of heart. And you shall sow your seed in vain, for your enemies shall eat it.'

When you walk in divine purpose, God will give rain in its season, the land shall yield produce, and the trees of the field shall yield their fruit.

Leviticus 26:3-4 (New King James Version)
'If you walk in My statutes and keep My commandments, and perform them, then I will give you rain in its season, the land shall yield its produce, and the trees of the field shall yield their fruit.'

Divine purpose connects with divine favour: divine favour is definitely undeserved when we look at it from the position of self righteousness. On the other hand, when we see the righteousness that has been imputed to us by the blood of Jesus, we will think otherwise. When God sees the blood, He sees Jesus, not us. The blood of Jesus is the conduit that connects our divine purpose with divine favour. Destined purpose is always divinely favoured. Even if it is popularly said that favour isn't fair, divine favour cannot locate those who trample on divine destiny. Divine favour is purposeful, it does not misfire.

1 Samuel 2:26 (New King James Version)
'And the child Samuel grew in stature, and in favor both with the LORD and men.'

When God favours you, men have no alternative but to also do the same. When you grow in stature, you will grow in favour. Stature is the degree of development and achievement attained. It is synonymous to qualification, development, competence, prominence, capacity, and eminence. Your stature is a link to your favour. You are hardly noticed if you have a small or average stature. Mediocrity is small and average. Your determination to achieve excellence in divine purpose increases your stature.

Luke 2:52 (New King James Version)
'And Jesus increased in wisdom and stature, and in favor with God and men.'

Wisdom, stature, and favour are connected. Wisdom makes you an extraordinary achiever. Achievement brings you honour before God and men. Wisdom increases your stature; your stature increases your favour.

Divine purpose creates a sustainable treasure and reward: staying put in your calling and achieving excellence in it, builds an enduring brand. An excellent brand stands the test of time. The time test is extremely fiery.

1 Corinthians 3:12-14 (New King James Version)
'Now if anyone builds on this foundation with gold, silver, precious stones, wood, hay, straw, each one's work will become clear; for the Day will declare it, because it will be revealed by fire; and the fire will test each one's work, of what sort it is. If anyone's work which he has built on it endures, he will receive a reward.'

If you're purpose driven, your work will come out purer and more treasured when taken through fire. Your brand is your work which will be made manifest on the last day. The more committed you are towards your goals, the more sustainable your treasures will be. For any treasure sustained, there is a reward obtained.

Divine purpose establishes your calling: to establish means, *'To install or settle in a position, place, business, etc.'* It also means, *'To show to be valid or true'*. When you're established, you are accepted and recognised. In establishment, you're enacted, appointed, and ordained for permanence.

1 Samuel 3:19-20 (New King James Version)
'So Samuel grew, and the LORD was with him and let none of his words fall to the ground. And all Israel from Dan to Beersheba knew that Samuel had been established as a prophet of the LORD.'

The key to establishment is growing in purpose. When you're growth driven, the Lord will be with you and establish you. You're not the one who will announce your establishment; it will be clear for everyone to see.

To secure your establishment in every sphere of life, growth is the answer. If you refuse to grow, you will be dwarfed by growing people. When you're dwarfed, you become inconspicuous.

Divine purpose sets you free from imprisonment: imprisonment is confinement, isolation, restraint, and duress. There are spiritual, mental, and physical imprisonments. In certain cases, there is a combination of two or three of them.

Whoever walks in purpose will always get delivered from the shackles of his enemies.

Acts 5:19-20 (New King James Version)
' But at night an angel of the Lord opened the prison doors and brought them out, and said, "Go, stand in the temple and speak to the people all the words of this life."'

If you 'do' God, no one can do away with you. I've heard some people say they neither 'do' God nor church. That is a statement of people without divine purpose. Those who don't 'do' God rot in spiritual and mental jails. If you refuse to acknowledge God as the truth, you cannot be set free. If you don't believe in God, He doesn't believe in you either. If you pitch your tent against your Maker, who will deliver you in the day of adversity? The end of the world is coming; there is a day of judgment when you can no longer run your mouth. When you meet death, you meet judgment. You can't come back to planet earth to repent folks! Watch your life!!

Isaiah 42:7 (New King James Version)
'To open blind eyes, to bring out prisoners from the prison, those who sit in darkness from the prison house.'

Acts 12:7 (New King James Version)
'Now behold, an angel of the Lord stood by him, and a light shone in the prison; and he struck Peter on the side and raised him up, saying, "Arise quickly!" And his chains fell off his hands.'

Divine purpose makes heaven your final home: after your work on earth, you will rest in the bosom of the Lord on your demise. There is no reward as big as making heaven. Nothing on earth is rewarding enough to take the place of being in the presence of the Lord. Heaven is lovely and peaceful.

Matthew 5:12 (New King James Version)
'Rejoice and be exceedingly glad, for great is your reward in heaven, for so they persecuted the prophets who were before you.'

There is a great reward in heaven for those who discover and follow their God-given purposes. If we suffer with Him, we shall also reign with Him. In suffering, we will have to drop our personal ambitions to follow His will. When we do, our blessings and rewards become eternal.

Heaven is real. Life after death is real. There are no regrets for those who embrace Jesus as the Way, the Truth, and the Life!

INHIBITORS OF PURPOSE

Inhibitors restrain, hinder, and prohibit an action and impulse. They decrease the rate of an action, and or, put a stop to your reaction. Inhibitors discourage, constrain, frustrate, obstruct, and suppress change. Inhibitors can be external or internal. It is external when it comes from outside, but internal when divine purpose is being crushed due to self-inflicting negative attitudes.

Some inhibitors of divine purpose are:

Wrong motive: motive is very broad, and as deep as the heart of man. Motive is a motivation. It is what causes a person to act in a certain way, or do certain things. Motive is the reason and prompting behind a motion. Most times, motives are hidden until they manifest.

The worst antagonist of divine purpose is wrong motive. If the reason for offering a divine service is based on self, greed, and personal gains, the service will not have a divine backing. When divine backing is missing, there won't be a divine covering.

Isaiah 14:12-15 (New King James Version)
'"How you are fallen from heaven, O Lucifer, son of the morning! How you are cut down to the ground, you who weakened the nations!

For you have said in your heart: ' I will ascend into heaven, I will exalt my throne above the stars of God; I will also sit on the mount of the congregation on the farthest sides of the north; I will ascend above the heights of the clouds, I will be like the Most High.' Yet you shall be brought down to Sheol, to the lowest depths of the Pit.'

There is danger in 'I', when it comes to divine purpose. If everything is centred on you, you will soon go down. Purpose is all about the One who gave it; God. The motto of divine purpose should read, *'For thine is the Kingdom, the power, and the glory. Forever and ever. Amen.'*

Lack of understanding: if you don't understand your vision, you cannot go on a mission. Divine purpose is intelligent. Mediocrity has no association with destiny. Ignorance is destructive. If you lack information, you cannot do well in your area of calling. Understanding is what keeps you abreast and puts you on top. You can't be knowledgeable and not perform excellently. In our callings, God expects nothing less than the best from us.

James 1:5 (New King James Version)
'Any of you lacks wisdom, let him ask of God, who gives to all liberally and without reproach, and it will be given to him.'

There is no harm in asking what you don't know. There is no shame in seeking understanding. Pride is the mother of assumption, presumption, and pretence. Holy Spirit, the Teacher is ever ready to pass quality information to those who are humble to learn. Admitting a lack of understanding is a qualitative attitude. Humble people will always emerge on top.

Habakkuk 2:2 (New King James Version)
'Then the LORD answered me and said: " Write the vision and make it plain on tablets, that he may run who reads it.'

Lazy people hate reading. If you hate reading, you will be

devoid of understanding. Reading a plain vision makes you run. Those who read it run while those who don't either stand still or join a race where they don't know its destination.

Using man as a standard: a standard is something considered by an authority or general consent as a basis of comparison. Standards are regarded as approved models.

Using man as a basis for spiritual standard is risky. A man is subject to errors and weaknesses. It is dangerous to make him a centre of focus when walking on the road of destiny.

Hebrews 12:2 (New King James Version)
'Looking unto Jesus, the author and finisher of our faith, who for the joy that was set before Him endured the cross, despising the shame, and has sat down at the right hand of the throne of God.'

The main definition of an author is, *'a creator or originator'*. A finisher is someone who brings something to an end or completion. No one can do the job of an author and a finisher except Jesus Christ. When you look unto Jesus, you see Jesus. Who you see is who your standard becomes. If you see man, your vision is earthly; if you see Jesus, it is heavenly. Those who see men look down but those who see Jesus look up. You can't look up and not go up.

Laziness and procrastination: laziness is lackadaisical, inattentive, indifferent, unconcerned, apathetic, lethargic, and somnolent. It averse or disinclines work or activity, thereby causing idleness and indolence.

Procrastination defers action. It delays an action until no action takes place. Procrastination is a self made devil that eats a person from the inside.

Laziness and procrastination are time thieves. Time is a depreciating asset in the hand of man. You can only enjoy it when you properly manage it. With time, the more you live, the less you're more likely to live. So, when you defer action, you waste life's essential asset. When you dawdle, you delay manifestation. Lazy and procrastinating people don't achieve divine purpose. They keep saying, 'I will' but never do. Lazy and indolent people are comparable to Lucifer who said, 'I will ascend into the heavens, I will exalt my throne, I will sit.' The devil kept saying, 'I will' until he was cast down. Just like the devil, lazy people dream unrealistic dreams. They build castles in the air and covet positions not meant for them. There is no chance in divine purpose for lazy people. There is no way in purpose for those who delay action. If God can't trust you with time, He can't trust you with destiny.

Romans 13:11-13 (New King James Version)
'And do this, knowing the time, that now it is high time to awake out of sleep; for now our salvation is nearer than when we first believed. The night is far spent, the day is at hand. Therefore let us cast off the works of darkness, and let us put on the armor of light. Let us walk properly, as in the day, not in revelry and drunkenness, not in lewdness and lust, not in strife and envy.'

Laziness and procrastination is darkness; hard work is light.

The love of money: the love of money is a profoundly tender and passionate affection for money. When the love of money becomes the purpose for pursuing divine destiny, the end becomes evil. The love of money kills visions and crumbles destiny.

2 Peter 2:15 (New King James Version)
'They have forsaken the right way and gone astray, following the way of Balaam the son of Beor, who loved the wages of unrighteousness;'

Jude 11 (New King James Version)
'Woe to them! For they have gone in the way of Cain, have run greedily in the error of Balaam for profit, and perished in the rebellion of Korah.'

2 Kings 5:26-27 (New King James Version)
'Then he said to him, "Did not my heart go with you when the man turned back from his chariot to meet you? Is it time to receive money and to receive clothing, olive groves and vineyards, sheep and oxen, male and female servants? Therefore the leprosy of Naaman shall cling to you and your descendants forever." And he went out from his presence leprous, as white as snow.'

The love of money aborts destinies. It's an impediment to mantle inheritance. Anyone who loves money passes on the legacy of leprosy. He passes generational curse down the line. Some of the leprous people in Israel were descendants of Gehazi. Some of them were probably among the people that Jesus healed. When money becomes the soul of a vision, the Spirit of fulfilment will be absent.

Haste and disobedience: haste is an unnecessary quick action based on thoughtlessness, rashness, and undue speed.

Disobedience is a refusal to comply. It disregards or transgresses against order. A disobedient person acts hastily. Haste and disobedience stampede destiny.

1Samuel 13:11-14 (New King James Version)
'And Samuel said, "What have you done?" Saul said, "When I saw that the people were scattered from me, and that you did not come within the days appointed, and that the Philistines gathered together at Michmash, then I said, 'The Philistines will now come down on me at Gilgal, and I have not made supplication to the LORD.' Therefore I felt compelled, and offered a burnt offering." And Samuel said to Saul, "You have done foolishly. You have not kept the commandment of the LORD your God, which He commanded you. For now the LORD would have established your kingdom over Israel forever. But now your kingdom shall not continue. The LORD has sought for Himself a man after His own heart, and the LORD has commanded him to be commander over His people, because you have not kept what the LORD commanded you."'

1 Samuel 15:22-23 (New King James Version)
'So Samuel said: "Has the LORD as great delight in burnt offerings and sacrifices, as in obeying the voice of the LORD? Behold, to obey is better than sacrifice, and to heed than the fat of rams. For rebellion is as the sin of witchcraft, and stubbornness is as iniquity and idolatry. Because you have rejected the word of the LORD, He also has rejected you from being king."'

Haste, if not promptly dealt with, graduates into disobedience. Disobedience leads to rejection. Disobedience encourages foolish decision making. Saul's obedience was partial; he destroyed the Amalekites but left the king of the Amalekites alive. Partial obedience is equivalent to disobedience. Saul killed the body but left the head alive. How can he not understand that killing the body and leaving the head alive is not death? When the head is alive, the body can regenerate.

Haste is the worst delay in life. Haste is the most expensive and wasteful item on earth. Haste is so costly that it can wipe away a whole nation. Haste plunders opportunities. Decisions made in a hurry end up in doom. If you plan in haste, it will end in hell. Haste and disobedience destroy destinies.

Pride: pride is a state of showing a high opinion of one's own dignity, importance, or superiority. Pride is a self image problem.

Proverbs 29:23 (New King James Version)
'A man's pride will bring him low, but the humble in spirit will retain honor.'

Pride dishonours the proud. It disgraces and forcefully reduces a person from something to nothing. Pride makes a person substandard and insignificant. A proud person is brought down below the generally accepted level. Shame and embarrassment is the end of a haughty man.

Proverbs 16:18-19 (New King James Version)
'Pride goes before destruction, and a haughty spirit before a fall.
Better to be of a humble spirit with the lowly, than to divide the spoil
with the proud.'

Pride precedes a fall. The fall of a proud person is not gentle; it is a crash. It is the crash that causes destruction. When something crashes, it is ripped in pieces. Anything inside something that crashes may perish with it. That is why it is vital that you avoid proud people. Pride destroys great purposes in life. Never entertain any form of it. Humility takes you to the top. Destiny is only fulfilled in the atmosphere of humbleness.

Wrong relationships: the word, *'relationship'* simply comes from the word, *'relation'*. It is a connection that forms an association. Every association has a bond or force of linkage. The bond of relationship is a property that associates two or more people in a definite order equally or unequally. Relationship is a principle, because it guides your rule of action or conduct. Your decisions, actions, and conducts are products of your relationship. Anyone you connect with walks into you, and you walk into that person. Relationship is infectious. When people connect with you, whatever they carry flows into you, and whatever you carry flows into them. Bridging the gap between you and someone creates a free flowing pathway between you and that person. So, you can easily flow into each other. Whoever you open the door of your heart to, becomes part of you. You are one with who you relate with.

Relationship must not be based on biological bloodline, but on divine purpose. A lot of people have perished because they never understood the principle of relationship. If you connect with people on the basis of familiarity, you may as well be connecting with familiar spirits. The new covenant redefined relationship, and made it more of spirituality than physicality.

141

Matthew 10:35-36 (New King James Version)
'For I have come to set a man against his father, a daughter against her mother, and a daughter-in-law against her mother-in-law'; and a man's enemies will be those of his own household.'

Who you love most is who you connect most with. Loving your nuclear family beyond the vision Giver attracts unworthiness. If your earthly bloodline does not embrace the principle of divine calling, your relationship must be ordinary. If it goes beyond that, your destiny will be scuffled.

Mark 10:7 (New King James Version)
'For this reason a man shall leave his father and mother and be joined to his wife.'

The new relationship leaves father and mother. Leaving father and mother does not mean not providing for them. Jesus rebuked the Pharisees for tithing but forsaking their parents. Leaving father and mother is a symbol of spiritual and mental maturity. The deep calls unto the deep. You are as deep or shallow as the person you relate with.

Relationships make you, and relationships destroy you. It depends on who you associate with.

1 Kings 12:13-14 (New King James Version)
'Then the king answered the people roughly, and rejected the advice which the elders had given him; and he spoke to them according to the advice of the young men, saying, "My father made your yoke heavy, but I will add to your yoke; my father chastised you with whips, but I will chastise you with scourges.'

As a result of wrong relationships, Rehoboam lost part of his kingdom and triggered a generational rebellion against the house of David. If you move with wrong people, you will be given wrong ideas. Wrong ideas produce wrong products. When you connect with people that disrespect value, you will lose part of your kingdom, if not all of it.

Comfort zone: a zone is a place of restriction. The state of ease and well being in a restricted place is a comfort zone. Dwelling in a comfort zone makes you avoid challenges. A comfortable attitude has a false image of having attained or achieved something. A comfortable attitude does not look up; it only sees its environment and levels lower than it. As a result, there is no inner drive to push up.

Philippians 3:12-14 (New King James Version)
'Not that I have already attained, or am already perfected; but I press on, that I may lay hold of that for which Christ Jesus has also laid hold of me. Brethren, I do not count myself to have apprehended; but one thing I do, forgetting those things which are behind and reaching forward to those things which are ahead, I press toward the goal for the prize of the upward call of God in Christ Jesus.'

A comfortable person feels he has reached the position of attainment and perfection. This character of contentment discourages a forward and upward advancement. When you're in a comfort zone, you think you have apprehended. Apprehension is a state of intuitive understanding. It is a level of full spiritual knowledge. To step out of your comfort zone, you must forget your achievements, and reach forward to those things which are ahead. There are lots of things ahead. Things ahead include the prize of the upward call of God in Christ Jesus. This shows that there are two types of calls; the lower call and the upward call. When you fulfil the lower call, you must press for the higher. Never settle for less.

Amos 6:1 (New King James Version)
'Woe to you who are at ease in Zion, and trust in Mount Samaria, notable persons in the chief nation, to whom the house of Israel comes!'

It is a dangerous trend to be at ease in Zion. Being at ease means you have no more dreams. Anyone who is at ease is calling for an untimely death. Being at ease means the person's vision on earth has finished. If a vision has ended, there is no reason to keep living because the essence of existence is vision.

143

Overburden and physical weariness: overburden and physical weariness make you lose focus. You can't be thorough when you're weary. Being thorough is what brings out the excellence in you. Physical and mental exhaustions reduce your level of concentration. If you can't concentrate, you can't be effective and produce an output of high efficiency.

Exodus 18:17-18 (New King James Version)
'So Moses' father-in-law said to him, "The thing that you do is not good. Both you and these people who are with you will surely wear yourselves out. For this thing is too much for you; you are not able to perform it by yourself."'

Putting too much on yourself isn't in your own interest. When you lose concentration, you misfire. Shooting off target does not make you achieve purpose. When you keep heaping too much on yourself, it will affect your health. Suffering from poor health is counter-productive.

Delegating duties eases burdens. Excellent human resources management is key to attaining a person's vision in life. Don't try to do what you're not trained for. Even if you were, if the responsibility is too huge, share it. Pay experts to help you. Don't bite off more than you can chew.

Assumption: assumption is a conclusion based on superficial evidence and the law of probability. It is a guess not a proof. Assumption is a sign of disconnection from the main source of information.

1 Samuel 1:12-15 (New King James Version)
'And it happened, as she continued praying before the LORD, that Eli watched her mouth. Now Hannah spoke in her heart; only her lips moved, but her voice was not heard. Therefore Eli thought she was drunk. So Eli said to her, "How long will you be drunk? Put your wine away from you!" But Hannah answered and said, "No, my lord, I am a woman of sorrowful spirit. I have drunk neither wine nor intoxicating drink, but have poured out my soul before the LORD.'

Assumption cannot discern the difference between drunkenness and a sorrowful spirit. Assumption cannot tell when a sorrowful heart is pouring out her soul before the Lord. Assumption makes wrong accusations.

When purpose is separated from inner vision, you cannot see beyond the façade. If you literarily understand the letter but not what is behind it, you will keep guessing. Assumption means, you've lost the inner sense of discernment and perception. Assumption and divine purpose do not match.

Dishonouring God: honour is a high respect for an object of integrity. When you dishonour a thing, you take away the worth, merit, or distinction. Dishonour reduces the ranking, title, and dignity of an object.

Dishonouring God is dishonouring your calling. You can't dishonour the Caller, and say, you respect the call. The Caller owns the call.

Matthew 6:13 (New King James Version)
'And do not lead us into temptation, but deliver us from the evil one. For Yours is the kingdom and the power and the glory forever. Amen.'

God owns the kingdom, the power of the kingdom, and the glory of the kingdom. He owns the offering and the sacrifice. He takes the responsibility and the praise. No one is big enough to compete or compare with him.

1 Samuel 2:29-30 (New King James Version)
'Why do you kick at My sacrifice and My offering which I have commanded in My dwelling place, and honor your sons more than Me, to make yourselves fat with the best of all the offerings of Israel My people?' Therefore the LORD God of Israel says: 'I said indeed that your house and the house of your father would walk before Me forever.' But now the LORD says: 'Far be it from Me; for those who honor Me I will honor, and those who despise Me shall be lightly esteemed.'

Dishonour takes away the best from God, and ascribes it to self. Dishonour is a misplacement of priorities, hierarchy, and heavenly vision. When you honour God, He will honour you. If you dishonour Him, He will dishonour you.

Dim vision: dim eyes don't see clearly. In dimness, there is no brightness, brilliance, or details. If you're dim, you suffer obscurity and indistinctiveness. A dim situation is unfavourable. A dim expectation is an expectation that is unlikely to happen or succeed.

There is danger in experiencing a dim vision. People with dim visions stumble and derail from their course.

1 Samuel 3:1-2 (New King James Version)
'Now the boy Samuel ministered to the LORD before Eli. And the word of the LORD was rare in those days; there was no widespread revelation. And it came to pass at that time, while Eli was lying down in his place, and when his eyes had begun to grow so dim that he could not see,'

When a vision is dim, the word of God will be rare. When a vision is dim, there will be no widespread revelation. A dim vision is downward fall. It terminates divine purpose abruptly. Dim visions make you lie down when you should be standing. It turns day into night, and night into outer darkness. When you experience a dim vision, you will feel the hand of Esau but hear the voice of Jacob. If you have a dim vision, the tendency of transferring a person's blessing to another individual becomes most probable.

Low sensitivity and perception to God's voice: sensitivity detects variation. Your ability to hear the still small voice depends on how sensitive you are to the things of the Spirit. If you cannot detect His voice, you cannot understand His words.

1 Samuel 3:8 (New King James Version)
'And the LORD called Samuel again the third time. So he arose and went to Eli, and said, "Here I am, for you did call me." Then Eli perceived that the LORD had called the boy.'

It took Eli three times to perceive the voice of God. He was supposed to be teaching young Samuel how to hear from God, but his low perception delayed his reception.

Low sensitivity and perception to spiritual things are big inhibitors of divine purpose. If you cannot hear clearly and promptly, you cannot move quickly. If you experience hard spiritual hearing, you need God's hearing aid; His word. Anyone who is deaf to His voice cannot walk in His purpose.

Wisdom hears promptly. Wisdom is sensitive to His voice. Embrace wisdom, and your ears will open widely to His counsel.

Lack of restraint: strain is a force that stretches a thing beyond the proper point or limit. When you restrain, you limit or hamper the activity, growth, or effect of a strain.

Restraint is a form of discipline. Restraining cuts down excesses. For instance, if a person wants to lose weight, he cuts down excessive eating. It takes a lot of self discipline to achieve that goal.

1 Samuel 3:13 (New King James Version)
'For I have told him that I will judge his house forever for the iniquity which he knows, because his sons made themselves vile, and he did not restrain them.'

Lack of restraint gives rise to a generational curse. Anyone who lacks spiritual restraint incurs the wrath of God's eternal judgment. Unborn generations can suffer from the carelessness of their ancestors if they lack spiritual understanding, whether born again or not. The truth you know is what sets you free.

147

Proverbs 29:18 (New King James Version)
'Where there is no revelation, the people cast off restraint; but happy is he who keeps the law.'

Eli's lack of revelation made the people cast off restraint. Where there is no restraint, there is no order. No one respects the law in a period of anarchy. Lack of restraint is an invitation to anarchy. Anarchy is lawlessness. Anyone is a leader where there is no control. Since Eli allowed his children to disrespect God's sacrifice, they went further in carrying the ark of the Lord without his permission. In the city of the blind, a one-eyed man is the king. It is vision that restrains. Where there is no vision, the people perish. Perishing is worse than mere dying. In ordinary death, the corpse is still intact, but in perishing, some body parts will be missing. The death of a visionless person is pathetic.

Family breakdown: when vehicles break down, they become immobile. No matter how expensive a vehicle may be, if it cannot move, it is not fit for purpose. A broken home is a broken vision. A home should be a family with one focus, but if the vision is broken by unnecessary distractions or interference, their goal cannot be achieved. A family goal is not an individualistic goal. It is a common goal achieved through a unification of forces.

In the western world especially, family breakdown, divorces, and separations have derailed the visions and expectations of many people. The ease with which families separate, with little consideration for the future of the children is alarming. Apart from separations, where there is no discipline in the home, the end product is the same.

1 Samuel 3:12-13 (New King James Version)
'In that day I will perform against Eli all that I have spoken concerning his house, from beginning to end. For I have told him that I will judge his house forever for the iniquity which he knows, because his sons made themselves vile, and he did not restrain them.'

148

A vile person is a wretchedly bad, highly offensive, unpleasant, and objectionable person. A vile person is repulsive, disgusting, morally debased, despicable, and degradable. These were the negative attributes of Hophni and Phinehas, but their father never restrained them.

If you cannot manage your home, you cannot manage divine purpose. If you condone family indiscipline and make excuses, your action will attract God's judgment. The ability to put one's home under control is a qualification for leadership. No one says it is easy, but if you're determined, prayerful, and ready to apply wisdom in correction, God will make a way. It takes a lot of mental and spiritual determination to raise a godly home. With patience and understanding, the vision to raise godly children is achievable.

Indifference: an indifferent attitude shows lack of concern or interest. Indifferent people disregard values, and consider them irrelevant.

1 Samuel 3:18 (New King James Version)
'Then Samuel told him everything, and hid nothing from him. And he said, "It is the LORD. Let Him do what seems good to Him."'

Indifference is a wrong response to an urgent challenge. An indifferent person is a lukewarm person; he is neither hot nor cold. An indifferent person is unmoved by an oncoming danger or rejection. It is not the attitude of faith to be indifferent. That is the mistake that some people make. They think faith is a state of indifference. No! Faith is active. Faith responds adequately to correct ugly situations. Faith does not allow destiny to slip off its hands. Faith protects the integrity of divine purpose. When faith receives a warning from God, it falls flat to ask for forgiveness. Faith is not careless, and does not talk carelessly. Faith does not disrespect Divinity.

Falling backward: your reaction to adversity is a reflection of your inherent character. Pressure releases your true identity.

1 Samuel 4:18a (New King James Version)
'Then it happened, when he made mention of the ark of God, that Eli fell off the seat backward by the side of the gate;'

Anyone who falls backward separates himself from divine purpose. In pursuance of destiny, the only alternative is to keep moving forward. Backsliders don't get to the finish line. The main reward of being in divine purpose is obtained at the end of the journey. When you fall, fall forward. Hezekiah fell forward, and was healed of his sickness. He had more years added to his life. Falling forward increases your longevity, but a backward fall brings death. Falling forward strengthens you; a backward fall breaks the neck.

Old age: some people are older than God in their own imaginations. They are too old to hear God's voice. They have stayed so long in the ministry that they don't need to hear God anymore. They've heard all they're supposed to hear and know all they're supposed to know.

1 Samuel 4:18b (New King James Version)
'.....and his neck was broken and he died, for the man was old '

Old age kills. An inability to renew your mind daily makes you old. If you rely on old information, you will become obsolete. Religion is an old age mentality.

Hebrews 10:19-20 (New King James Version)
'Therefore, brethren, having boldness to enter the Holiest by the blood of Jesus, by a new and living way which He consecrated for us, through the veil, that is, His flesh.'

There is a new and living way. Forsaking this way and holding on to rigidity is deadly. Jesus has provided pure water that washes and renews us daily. We don't have to look spiritually ragged to show how much we love Him. Revelation knowledge is the pure water that cleanses us from the old methods of living and making decisions.

Heavy weight: a heavy weight limits flexibility, thereby slowing down movement. Whether physically, mentally, or spiritually, too much weight kills. When you're too heavy to pray, or too heavy to hear God, divine purpose will be punctured.

A heavy weight does not respond easily to God's stimulus. A heavy weight attitude is one of complete arrogance towards spiritual issues.

1 Samuel 4:18 (New King James Version)
'Then it happened, when he made mention of the ark of God, that Eli fell off the seat backward by the side of the gate; and his neck was broken and he died, for the man was old and heavy. And he had judged Israel forty years.'

It was Eli's weight that killed him. Heavy weight kills; please humble yourself. If you're too high, come down. If a person chooses to remain high on his own accord, the impact of his fall will be devastating. God save the person if he falls on a concrete floor. Most heavy weights fall on concrete floors.

Humility is the key to sustaining a divine position. God elevates those who are low in their eyes. It is not the will of God for any to fall. If we shed weight, we will live longer.

DIMENSIONAL PURPOSE

Apart from the mathematical meanings and applications of dimension, it also means UNIT. Unit means ONE. Unit is single, individualistic, specific, and entity.

In sports, there are team games, and there are also games for individuals. In a team game, everyone makes his or her individual contribution targeted towards a victory. The strength of a team is a sum of the strength of the individuals who make up the team. A weak link in that chain reduces the chances of a victory. In team games, it easy to cover up weakness, but in individual games, you can't.

Life is more serious than a game, because one's attitude to life is what determines the ability to win a game. Life without purpose is life without reason. Purpose is collective and individualistic. An individual's contribution to a collective purpose is dimensional purpose. In a team, you must make an impact and that impact must be from the heart of total commitment. A contribution that is not total is an unacceptable commitment. It is not commitment until it is one hundred percent. Commitment is wholesome; wholesomeness involves the spiritual, mental, and physical realms. A commitment that does not involve the totality of the spirit, soul and body is hypocritical. Dimensional purpose defines an individual's purpose in a main purpose. The main purpose is the big picture. The big picture is God's divine intention for the Church. You are held responsible for your share of the big picture.

Galatians 6:5 (God's Word)
'Assume your own responsibility'

Your responsibility is your individual purpose. You cannot shift it. If you abandon it, it will be there waiting for you. Your divine purpose is your burden, share, and load. When you make your burden your goal, you will have no time for frivolities. You must take upon yourself the divine duties that God has delegated to you. It is your responsibility.

Matthew 25:18 (New King James Version)
'But he who had received one went and dug in the ground, and hid his lord's money.'

If someone 'went', it means the person has strength. You can't move without energy. If you have the energy to move, you should also have the strength to apply appropriately the talent you've been given. Moving in the wrong direction for the wrong action is a misappropriation of divine gifting. A person who can dig the ground definitely has some skills. A person who can hide money for a long time has some banking or financial skills. For the man with one talent, it wasn't a case of deficiency of skills or innovation, but an outright wickedness coupled with a wrong character. Wrong characters don't invest their divine gifts. They preserve talent until it is taken away from them. Wrong characters waste useful time. They sit down to create rhetorical excuses that could win a modern day law suit in a high court, yet, never apply that rhetoric in business planning and marketing.

The man with one talent wasn't a bad team player. If he was, he would have been fired long before. He was just someone who couldn't stand on his own feet. He had a character of dependency. He could work in a team, but couldn't for himself. His dependency trait robbed him the opportunity to manage his own business. Apart from failing as a sole proprietor, he also failed in communication skills.

The inability to invest a blessing halts procreativity. It is wickedness not to be a profit minded person. A saver mentality is a lazy mentality. Investors take risk and make profits; savers conserve and make interest. However, interest is peanuts when compared to the profits made by those who invest.

Matthew 25:24-25 & 30 (New King James Version)
'"Then he who had received the one talent came and said, 'Lord, I knew you to be a hard man, reaping where you have not sown, and gathering where you have not scattered seed. And I was afraid, and went and hid your talent in the ground. Look, there you have what is yours. .....And cast the unprofitable servant into the outer darkness. There will be weeping and gnashing of teeth.'

If a saver mentality is a lazy mentality, how much more a hiding mentality. A person with an idle and hidden talent is lazy and wicked. Talent laundering is worse than money laundering. The people who hide talents are unprofitable, and will be cast into outer darkness where there will be weeping and gnashing of teeth. Some outer darkness may not necessarily be hell, but the severe consequences of not living in divine purpose. Lack, poverty, sicknesses and diseases, unfulfilled dreams, and other negative consequences constitute outer darkness. The pain of living from hand to mouth is a product of outer darkness. The hurt of being materially full and spiritually empty is outer darkness.

There is peace in finding real purpose. There is satisfaction in fulfilling it. The reward of walking in real purpose cannot be over-emphasised. When you follow the reason for living, you will become the reason for existence. You are a divine reason when you pursue divine purpose.

See yourself as a reason, because that's what you are. See yourself as a destiny, that's what you are. Drive yourself into the future, you've got the vigour.

GOALS IN DIMENSIONAL PURPOSE

What is life without goals? Life has no meaning if it cannot be defined. Goals define existence. There would be nothing to work for, if there is nothing to expect. Expectation is the soul of existence. The goal for driving a car is destination. Those who go on jolly rides cause severe accidents. If you're being driven to no destination, you will unnecessarily wear yourself out. When you're in a race, what is your motive? If you're running without a prize, it is an exercise in futility. Futility is not result oriented. It is ineffective, useless, and unsuccessful. As an individual, your dimensional purpose must have goals and objectives. When you follow the goals of destiny, you will reap the rewards of destiny. Your goals must be immediate and futuristic, small and massive.

Family goals: a family is a basic social unit consisting of parents (married male and female) and their children, considered as a group, whether dwelling together or not. It is also a social unit consisting of one or two adults together with the children they care for, as in the case of single parents. Although there are other definitions of family, which include descendants of a common progenitor, my focus is on the nuclear family; parent (s) and their children. The children include those adopted or being cared for.

Anyone who assumes the headship of a home must set family goals. The family is the root of the entire society. If the root is rotten, it cannot absorb adequate nutrients for the growth of the plant. If quality and sufficient nutrients are not absorbed, the plant will die. When plants die, they cause a shortage in food supply. No food no life.

1 Corinthians 11:3 (New King James Version)
'But I want you to know that the head of every man is Christ, the head of woman is man, and the head of Christ is God. '

If you replace the word, *'Head'* with *'Responsibility'*, the above passage will read, *'But I want you to know that the responsibility of every man is Christ, the responsibility of woman is man, and the responsibility of Christ is God.'*

Headship is a responsibility. A position calls for responsibilities. The head of any organisation takes responsibility for that organisation. Personalities make up organisations, and in an organisation, there must be a chain of authority. This chain of authority called an organisational chart defines every member's position and responsibilities. Headship is not a verbal utterance, but a position that requires actions in provisions, protection, and other responsibilities tied to the office.

Where there are two parents, the head of the family is the man, otherwise whoever is present out of the two (male or female) takes responsibilities. Taking responsibilities does not only involve physical provisions, but also spiritual and mental well being.

1 Timothy 5:8 (New King James Version)
'But if anyone does not provide for his own, and especially for those of his household, he has denied the faith and is worse than an unbeliever.'

'Anyone' includes father, mother, and single parents. Inasmuch as you're responsible for a household, you fall into the category of *'anyone'*. Provision is not only materialistic. The order of importance of provision starting from the highest is spiritual, mental, and physical. Faith is a spiritual action. If anyone does not provide for his own household, he has denied the faith. If you understand spirituality, it will be easier for you to deal with mentality and physicality. A man who claims to know God but does not give his family a wholesome provision is an unbeliever. There are many prayerful unbelievers who are worse than infidels.

There is no divine purpose that has no plan for the family. Any purpose that does not take the family into consideration is heading downward. Purpose does not disconnect a family, it brings them together. Your home is the foundation of your purpose. Your journey always begins from home. The idea for the business that gave you so much money began from home. At least, some of your business plans were written on the dining table. Some of the ideas inputted into those great plans came from your spouse or children. Never ignore the agents of a small beginning.

Your family goals in your divine purpose must include:

<u>Love</u>

Ephesians 5:25 (New King James Version)
'Husbands, love your wives, just as Christ also loved the church and gave Himself for her,'

The Bible did not say, *'Husband, love your wives'*. Marital love is unitary, not pluralistic. If you love your wife, you will definitely love your children. The procedure for family love is husband loving wife first, and then the children follow, not vice versa. Some husbands prefer their children to their wives. This is not biblical.

<u>Blessing</u>

Genesis 48:20 New King James Version)
'So he blessed them that day, saying, "By you Israel will bless, saying, 'May God make you as Ephraim and as Manasseh!'" And thus he set Ephraim before Manasseh.'

Your dimensional purpose includes blessing your family, not cursing them. You cannot pronounce blessings and curses from the same mouth. A blessing is a seed sown in the life of someone. Blessings come in form of words. Whatever you pronounce on your family, will germinate after a period of time. You can't plant the wrong seed and expect a good fruit. You only reap what you sow. Sow blessings and you will reap a bumper harvest of blessings.

Inheritance

Proverbs 13:22 (New King James Version)
'A good man leaves an inheritance to his children's children, but the wealth of the sinner is stored up for the righteous.'

Two generations after you, are your children's children. For a man to leave an inheritance for his grandchildren, he must have done two things; leave an inheritance for his immediate children, and teach them management and investment principles that will multiply the inheritance, so that his grandchildren can benefit from it. Leaving an inheritance for your children's children makes you a good man.

Provision

1 Timothy 5:8 (New King James Version)
'But if anyone does not provide for his own, and especially for those of his household, he has denied the faith and is worse than an unbeliever.'

The King James Version calls an unbeliever, an infidel. An infidel is a person who disbelieves or doubts a particular theory, belief, creed, etc. An infidel is agnostic, atheist, heathen, or heretic. A man who does not provide for his household is worse than an atheist.

Physical presence

Leviticus 25:10 (New King James Version)
'And you shall consecrate the fiftieth year, and proclaim liberty throughout all the land to all its inhabitants. It shall be a Jubilee for you; and each of you shall return to his possession, and each of you shall return to his family.'

'Each of you shall return to his family'. There is the need for a parental physical presence in the family, especially the father. There is jubilee in returning home. A jubilee brings jubilation. A jubilant family is a joyful family.

Standing in the gap

Ezekiel 22:30 (New King James Version)
'So I sought for a man among them who would make a wall, and stand in the gap before Me on behalf of the land, that I should not destroy it; but I found no one.'

In your family, you must make a wall, and stand in the gap. This is part of the responsibility of headship. A gap is a break or opening, as in a fence, wall, or military line. It is an empty space or interval that interrupts continuity. When you stand in the gap, you block every exposure or leakage that causes unnecessary entry and exit. The one who stands in the gap takes the heat and the punches. It takes a fighter to stand in the gap. It takes a tolerant and resistant person to stand in the gap. When you stand in the gap, what created the loophole will come after you. It will test your character, strategic warfare and resilience. When you stand your ground, it will flee, but if you waver, you won't only be knocked down and out, but a bigger gap will be created, making the situation worse.

Sacrifice

Sacrifice is self denial. A visionary must be a person of sacrifice. Sacrifice for your family is the first test in divine purpose.

John 13:14 (New King James Version)
'If I then, your Lord and Teacher, have washed your feet, you also ought to wash one another's feet.'

Sacrifice comes down to washing feet. If you can't come down, you can't calm down. Sacrifice emaciates. It takes the best out of you, and sows it. When you sacrifice, it appears like all is lost, but the rewards come in multiples.

A custodian of the ark

1 Chronicles 13:14 (New King James Version)
'The ark of God remained with the family of Obed-Edom in his house

160

three months. And the LORD blessed the house of Obed-Edom and all that he had.'

The ark of God denotes His presence. The ark of God resides in His temple, and His temple is you. It is your responsibility to maintain God's presence in your family. The presence of God in a home brings blessings upon that home.

Refuge

Proverbs 14:26 (New King James Version)
'In the fear of the LORD there is strong confidence, and His children will have a place of refuge.'

A refuge is a shelter or protection from trouble or danger. It is a place of aid, relief, and escape. When you make God your place of refuge, you'll become a protection for your family.

Glory

Proverbs 17:6 (New King James Version)
'Children's children are the crown of old men, and the glory of children is their father.'

A glory is a source of honour, fame, and admiration. It is a state of great splendour, magnificence, prosperity, absolute happiness, gratification, and radiance. The glory of children must be their father. It is your responsibility to make your family shine. If your family isn't shining, you're not glowing. Glory glows!

Instruction

Proverbs 4:1 (New King James Version)
'Hear, my children, the instruction of a father, and give attention to know understanding;'

Instruction is the act of imparting knowledge or information. It is the responsibility of the head of the household to instruct the children. Instructions correct, reprove, and enlighten.

Training and admonition

Ephesians 6:4 (New King James Version)
'And you, fathers, do not provoke your children to wrath, but bring them up in the training and admonition of the Lord.'

Training is related to development, proficiency, practice, and performance. Admonition cautions, advises, counsels, reproves, or scolds. Provocation incites, instigates, angers, and irritates. Provocation produces wrath. Wrath is a strong, stern, and fierce anger. It is a deeply resentful indignation.

Provocation is not training, it is an abuse. It is a wrong communication strategy in raising a child.

Discipline

Proverbs 19:18 (New King James Version)
'Chasten your son while there is hope, and do not set your heart on his destruction.'

To *'set your heart on his destruction'* means to give up hope. It is an attitude of mental laziness. Discipline is painful because it makes you stick to a defined set of rules, but the rewards are immense. Rules must not always favour children. Cutting down excesses is discipline. Excesses include spending long hours in front of the television or internet.

The goals of a calling: a calling is a strong impulse or inclination to a trade, profession, mission, pursuit, field, specialty, vocation, or convocation. A call is summon and an order to divine duty.

Matthew 20:8-16 (New King James Version)
'"So when evening had come, the owner of the vineyard said to his steward, 'Call the laborers and give them their wages, beginning

with the last to the first.' And when those came who were hired about the eleventh hour, they each received a denarius. But when the first came, they supposed that they would receive more; and they likewise received each a denarius. And when they had received it, they complained against the landowner, saying, 'These last men have worked only one hour, and you made them equal to us who have borne the burden and the heat of the day.' But he answered one of them and said, 'Friend, I am doing you no wrong. Did you not agree with me for a denarius? Take what is yours and go your way. I wish to give to this last man the same as to you. Is it not lawful for me to do what I wish with my own things? Or is your eye evil because I am good?' So the last will be first, and the first last. For many are called, but few chosen.'''

From the human angle, this parable is not based on the principle of fairness. How can one be called to work from the early hours of the morning but receive the same wages with someone who worked for just one hour? As with any parable given by Jesus Christ, there are deep truths hidden within.

Before a call, God looks at the willingness, readiness, and swiftness of a person's response to a call. Your willingness, readiness, and swiftness compensates for time wasted. In the above Bible passage, it is written, 'And about the eleventh hour he went out and found others standing idle'. The eleventh hour labourers, despite a long wait, were still standing and hoping that somehow, they too would get a job. Their eleventh hour faith was what gave them a day's wages. Some of their colleagues would have given up, and gone back home, but they kept waiting until a miracle happened. While waiting, they kept standing. Some of their mates who waited by sitting down were not hired. Their determination and ability to wait for hours in discomfort gave them an unusual breakthrough. It is your determination to never give up your dreams and visions that makes you chosen. Even if you're a last comer, the accumulation of your positive character and your zeal to beat limitations and the stress of long wait will give you the same reward as those who have worked since morning. While you wait, you must not sit but keep standing. Your standing will make the landowner spot you. If you sit in a marketplace, no one will identify you. The marketplace is rowdy, noisy, and packed full. It takes those who are standing to be noticed. If you're not noticed by the landowner, you cannot be hired. The type of person who notices you determines your level of provision. Landowners are wealthy people; they carry wages in their hands. Remember, 'The earth is the Lord's'. He is the Landowner. If God recognises you, you're made. Keep standing. Keep trusting. Keep believing.

In your calling, some of the things you must avoid are: complaining against God, supposition, wrong negotiation, and an evil eye. In the parable of the labourers, all the labourers that were hired early in the morning complained but only one was spotted out because of his evil eye. The passage reads, 'But he answered one of them and said…Or is your eye evil because I am good?' We should realise that experience doesn't make a man chosen, it is commitment that does.

In your calling, you must:

Seek the anointing

If you're called to be a civil engineer, when the anointing rests on you, you will design what no man has ever done. The anointing, which is a divine enablement will give you uniqueness in your purpose.

John 14:26 (New King James Version)
'But the Helper, the Holy Spirit, whom the Father will send in My name, He will teach you all things, and bring to your remembrance all things that I said to you.'

The anointing is a Helper. The Helper teaches you all things and reminds you all things that He has said to you. To remind means to 'RE-MIND', that is, to repeat it to the mind. The anointing repeats positive ideas in your mind, even if you've forgotten. The Holy Spirit teaches you the skills of a profession if you yield to Him.

Write it down

Whatever is unwritten cannot be used as a document. Written words, dreams, visions, and purposes are substances, evidences, and documents of faith. Jesus referred to what was written when He was tempted by the devil. What you've written is what you refer to when the going gets rough and tough. In life, the going sometimes get tough. When it does, you can go back and read those visions that God put in your spirit. Reading them again encourages you in times of difficulties.

Visions multiply through the process of being written down. When you learn to write down divine and useful information, revelations, and expectations, you will have something to put God in remembrance.

Revelation 1:11 (New King James Version)
'Saying, "I am the Alpha and the Omega, the First and the Last," and, "What you see, write in a book and send it to the seven churches which are in Asia: to Ephesus, to Smyrna, to Pergamos, to Thyatira, to Sardis, to Philadelphia, and to Laodicea."'

You must see, write, and send; seeing, writing, and sending takes a vision beyond self. Writing makes sure that the generations after you benefit from your vision.

Speak out

People may not like your accent, tone, or grammatical errors, but still speak out. An unspoken vision is an unfulfilled vision. Make noise about your calling. Some may resent your boldness, it doesn't matter. If you don't market your vision, no one will buy it. You're the main person responsible for advertising what you carry within you. What is the use of a good product if people don't know it exists? Even if God reveals you, you must also take steps to reveal yourself. You reveal yourself by speaking your dreams and visions. When you're enthusiastic about your divine purpose, you incite other people to embrace it.

Proverbs 6:2 (New King James Version)
'You are snared by the words of your mouth; you are taken by the words of your mouth.'

A snare is anything that traps or entangles someone or something unawares. The words you speak into the air will return back to trap or entangle you unawares. Imagine yourself speaking your visions, dreams, and divine purpose, one day while you're unaware, the results of those words will come back to trap or entangle you.

'To be taken' means *'To be caught'*. I want to be caught by the words of divine purpose. I want to be entangled by the words of divine purpose.

Anger

Proverbs 15:1 (New King James Version)
'A soft answer turns away wrath, but a harsh word stirs up anger.'

There are two types of anger; the one that sins and the one that sins not. The one that sins is negative; the one that doesn't is inspiring. Anger is like still waters that are only stirred up by harsh words. There are certain situations in life where a person needs to trouble that anger in order to get an inspiring result. If you're at ease when you should be moving, you must as a matter of compulsion, either say some harsh words to yourself or listen to someone say it directly to you. If you cannot rouse yourself from inactivity, quiet, contentment, and indifference, you will find yourself in a condition of lukewarmness.

Anger gets you out of your comfort zone. It makes you see the empty space in front of you. Anger takes away from you *'the achiever'* mentality, and puts a new hunger in you. Be angry; be positively angry.

Drive yourself

Divine timing generates anger; anger generates drive. Drive is kinetic, motional, and accelerating.

Mark 1:12 (New King James Version)
' Immediately the Spirit drove Him into the wilderness.'

I like drive. What can a person achieve without drive? Nothing! Before you can be driven into the city, you must first be driven into the wilderness. If you can't face the test of the wilderness, you can't pass the test of the city. If you can't manage the wilderness, you can't manage the pressure of the city. Those who overcome the temptations of the wilderness prevail over the cross. There is a cross for every call. There is a pain for every divine purpose. Drive makes the weight on the way become lighter. Drive does not stop the tempter, it is the written word that does. Drive does not make angels minister to you, it is your overcoming experience that does. Drive takes you to the wilderness, but your understanding preserves you.

Never change the direction where the Holy Spirit drives you. Never complain when your hunger produces a temptation. For every hunger, there is a tempter. For every temptation you overcome, there are heavenly ministers who attend to you.

Strength

Matthew 14: 21-23 (New King James Version)
'Now those who had eaten were about five thousand men, besides women and children. Immediately Jesus made His disciples get into the boat and go before Him to the other side, while He sent the multitudes away. And when He had sent the multitudes away, He went up on the mountain by Himself to pray. Now when evening came, He was alone there.'

167

The physical strength of Jesus Christ is humanly unimaginably crazy. To host 5,000 men in one evening, and then, still go to the mountain to pray all night is incredible. Jesus dished the meal all alone, and gave to the disciples to serve the multitude. This is a display of unusual strength. Women can appreciate better what Jesus did that night. Hosting a hundred people in one evening is enough trouble for the night, let alone 5,000. To fulfil your divine purpose, you need unusual strength.

Romans 8:11 (New King James Version)
'But if the Spirit of Him who raised Jesus from the dead dwells in you, He who raised Christ from the dead will also give life to your mortal bodies through His Spirit who dwells in you.'

The Holy Spirit gives physical strength. When you depend on Him, He will give strength to your physical bodies. You can't fulfil purpose without the help of the Holy Spirit. If you rely on your own strength, you will breakdown in no time, but when you depend on Him, you will exhibit a strength that exceeds your imagination. The exhibition of strength does not mean lack of rest. When the body needs rest, give it some. Not taking rest is counter productive.

Keep learning

When you continue to be a baby in God's hands, He will continue to teach you. When you keep learning, you will keep growing. You are as big as the information you ingest. You are as precious and fresh as the spiritual meal you eat. Under no circumstance should a person stop learning. Never stop learning; stoop to learn.

2 Timothy 4:13 (New King James Version)
'Bring the cloak that I left with Carpus at Troas when you come—and the books, especially the parchments.'

A parchment is the skin of sheep, goat, etc prepared for use as a material on which to write. It is also a manuscript or document on such material.

Never forget the books and the parchments. The parchment is very relevant because that is where revelations are written. Don't write down on patches, write on parchments.

Education goals: divine purpose does not accommodate illiteracy. The Bible completely abhors it.

Acts 17:30 (The Message)
'God overlooks it as long as you don't know any better—but that time is past. The unknown is now known, and he's calling for a radical life-change.'

The New Testament dispensation does not condone ignorance; whether secular, mental, or spiritual. God is calling the Church for a radical life change as far as educational goals are concerned. God does not overlook ignorance. Ignorance makes the Church look stupid, cheap, and ludicrous. The Bible is an embodiment of mysteries, and it takes divine knowledge to decipher what is written. Seeking the depth of this knowledge unravels the pictures behind the wall. The wall is the letter, and the picture is the revelation. If you don't break down the wall, you can't walk into the throne room. In the throne room is the real deal. It takes undaunted diligence to breakdown the parables in order to go beyond any paradox.

2 Timothy 2:15 (New King James Version)
'Be diligent to present yourself approved to God, a worker who does not need to be ashamed, rightly dividing the word of truth.'

Studying requires diligence. Diligence is a constant and earnest effort to accomplish what is undertaken, that is, a persistent exertion of spirit, mind, and body. It is also the degree of care and caution required by the circumstances of a person. The characteristics of diligence include application, attention, intensity, activity, exertion, and intent.

An approval is a formal consent or confirmation. It is a certification of agreement that makes you qualify for a study undertaken. God approves a diligent person who rightly divides the word of truth.

Acts 4:13 (New King James Version)

'Now when they saw the boldness of Peter and John, and perceived that they were uneducated and untrained men, they marveled. And they realized that they had been with Jesus.'

You can't be with Jesus and remain ignorant. For about three years of Jesus' Ministry on earth, His illiterate disciples embarked on a wholesome study in the best one on one University that the world had, and can ever offer. Jesus taught them day and night. He taught them spiritual, mental, and physical education. He turned them from ignorant people to Preachers, Teachers, Lawyers, Business Consultants, Physicians, etc. In recent years, I have heard of people who couldn't read or write, but in looking into the Bible daily, started learning to read and write. Today, some of them are intellectuals.

There is no excuse for not having an educational purpose. An unstudied purpose is an unfulfilled purpose. If you're not growing mentally, you can't grow spiritually. When Peter stood at the temple, and before the Sanhedrin to defend the healing of the lame man at the beautiful gate, he used a communication model known as the rhetorical model. In the rhetorical model, you defend a case by citing a historical background to back up your argument. This is one of the methods used by Lawyers in dealing with cases. He was an uneducated and illiterate man, who out of the character of diligence studied to show himself approved to God. The defence method adopted by Peter was the same approach used by Apostle Paul when he stood before Festus and King Agrippa. One can argue that Paul was a Lawyer. Was Peter also a Lawyer? One can also argue that the Holy Ghost told Peter what to say. Yes, you're right, but read this!

John 14:25-26 (New King James Version)
'These things I have spoken to you while being present with you.
But the Helper, the Holy Spirit, whom the Father will send in My
name, He will teach you all things, and bring to your remembrance
all things that I said to you.'

'He will teach you all things, and bring to your remembrance all
things that I said to you.' It takes a teachable spirit to be taught.
You cannot be reminded of what you haven't studied. The
Holy Spirit goes into history to remind you the knowledge
you have acquired in the past. If you have no account of
knowledge, you cannot withdraw information from an empty
treasury.

The Holy Spirit only teaches those who have the hunger for
information. How far can you go with your dreams and
visions, if you don't know what it entails? God gives the
vision; you're responsible for making it become flesh.
Information, knowledge, wisdom, etc are the cells that fuse
together to create the reality of purpose. If you have no goal for
education, you have no goal for divine purpose. Wholesome
education is purpose preparation.

Career, profession, and business goals: there is career,
profession, and business in dimensional purpose.

A career is a success in a profession or occupation. It is a person's
progress or general course of action through life or a phase
of life, as in some profession or undertaking. It involves specialty,
procedure, vocation, and progress.

A profession is a body of persons engaged in an occupation
or calling. Your profession is your confession.

A business encompasses careers, professions, and all activities
and resources involved in a profit-seeking enterprise or
concern.

Proverbs 24:3-4 (Living Bible)
'Any enterprise is built by wise planning, becomes strong through common sense, and profits wonderfully by keeping abreast of the facts.'

The goal of divine purpose must be a career goal, with the intention of developing it into an enterprise. An enterprise is a project or undertaking that requires boldness or effort and the readiness to embark on new ventures and initiatives. Every enterprise has a motivation; profits. Profits are not only materialistic but three dimensional; spiritual, mental, and physical.

Proverbs 14:23 (New King James Version)
'In all labor there is profit, but idle chatter leads only to poverty.'

There is profit in all labour, whether in the spiritual, mental, or physical dimension. Anyone who says he doesn't like profits is a liar. Some people are too spiritual to talk about financial profits; meanwhile, in the depth of their hearts, the voice of money speaks so loud.

In any career, there is a progression. Progression requires development. Development is a growth or expansion that brings a person or a thing to a more advanced and effective state. You can't walk in divine purpose without growing in it. Purpose is not stagnant but motional. Purpose moves or progresses by wise planning, common sense, and keeping abreast of the facts. The facts are quality information. Quality information requires quality investment in career building. To get the best answers, you must ask the best people. To get the best people, you must invest in the best places. Information that grows divine purpose is never cheap. You must work long and in unusual hours to get unusual information. You must spend an unusual amount of money to buy quality knowledge. You must subscribe for the best career building journals to obtain cutting edge information. Remember, *'Through wisdom a house is built, and by understanding it is established; by knowledge the rooms are filled with all precious and pleasant riches.'*

Leadership goals: great leadership imbibes great wisdom. Wisdom applies divine knowledge to solve very difficult problems. Wisdom and smartness are completely opposite. Wisdom adopts divine rules; smartness uses human reasoning. Wisdom dissolves predicaments; smartness tries to corner them. The solution proffered by wisdom is permanent; smartness gives temporal solutions.

Proverbs 4:7 (New King James Version)
'Wisdom is the principal thing; therefore get wisdom. And in all your getting, get understanding.'

A principal is the first and highest in rank, importance, and value. It is the chief or head, and a person who takes a leading role or part in any activity.

In pursuing divine purpose, you must be determined to be the head in what you do. A head takes responsibilities in an outstanding way. To be a principal, wisdom must live and walk with you. Anyone who wants to be head must embrace God's wisdom. Embracing God's wisdom puts you in the position of creative and innovative leadership. Creative and innovative leadership puts you on top in whatever you do. When you're on top, you're the best. When you're the best, you also earn the best. Your earning in whatever capacity it comes is a reward for being diligent in your calling. Diligent people don't sit with mere men; they sit with kings. If you want to sit with kings, possess wisdom. Wisdom is the principal thing; wisdom is the head. In life, wisdom will continue to be the head.

Mark 9:35 (New King James Version)
'And He sat down, called the twelve, and said to them, "If anyone desires to be first, he shall be last of all and servant of all."'

As a servant, you don't serve yourself first before others. You're the last to be served. A servant is a person in the service of another; he's an assistant, attendant, and a helper.

Deuteronomy 28:13 (New King James Version)
'And the LORD will make you the head and not the tail; you shall be above only, and not be beneath, if you heed the commandments of the LORD your God, which I command you today, and are careful to observe them.'

Heeding is heading, and heading involves careful observation. The key to headship is heeding the commandments of God with careful and cautious observations. The head and the tail belong to one body. Heads don't move alone, neither do tails. The position you occupy is determined by your level of obedience. Some people are neither head nor tail. They are in the middle of the road. People with undefined obedience occupy undefined positions. When you heed, you head.

Life after death goals: the plan for divine purpose must include where you will spend eternity. If you don't plan for life after death, your purpose is carnal. To be carnally minded is death, but to be spiritually minded is life and peace. Purpose ends in eternity.

Revelation 21:1-5 (New King James Version)
'Now I saw a new heaven and a new earth, for the first heaven and the first earth had passed away. Also there was no more sea. Then I, John, saw the holy city, New Jerusalem, coming down out of heaven from God, prepared as a bride adorned for her husband. And I heard a loud voice from heaven saying, "Behold, the tabernacle of God is with men, and He will dwell with them, and they shall be His people. God Himself will be with them and be their God. And God will wipe away every tear from their eyes; there shall be no more death, nor sorrow, nor crying. There shall be no more pain, for the former things have passed away." Then He who sat on the throne said, "Behold, I make all things new." And He said to me, "Write, for these words are true and faithful."'

The whole essence of divine purpose is a shambles if a person gains the whole world and loses his soul. Being an inhabitant of the new heaven and new earth is divine purpose made completely perfect. When the earth melts away, and the heavens are folded like a piece of paper, where will you be? There are just two options; heaven and hell. Heaven is new, hell is old. Any place that is new is fresh, innovating, and creative. Old places are obsolete, wasted, and unfit for purpose. An eternal purpose embraces eternal life. Earthly purpose embraces limitations and death. Those who choose life make Jesus their Lord and personal Saviour, and they walk in the dictates and principles of the heavenly kingdom. The power to decide your destiny lies with you. Your power is your choice. Choice is a destination and destination is a choice. Confessing Jesus as Lord and Saviour is the best profession that man can ever utter out of his mouth. Those who speak Jesus speak life. Saying anything else is detrimental to your life.

CONCLUSION

Ecclesiastes 12:13-14 (New King James Version)
'Let us hear the conclusion of the whole matter: Fear God and keep His commandments, for this is man's all. For God will bring every work into judgment, including every secret thing, whether good or evil.'

A conclusion is a final decision, judgement, resolution, admission, or an end of a matter or issue. The fear of God and obedience to His commandments is the summary of a man's purpose on earth. Purpose will be judged, whether good or evil. The secrecy behind purpose will be taken through the fire. If the motive behind it is good, it will pass the test of the flame, but if not, it will become ashes. Ashes don't give rewards. Ashes are for mourners.

It is better to hear the conclusion of a matter from the beginning than wait for the end before being granted access to the information. When you know the conclusion, you picture the expectation. Destiny is an expectation. Your destiny should be a good secret revealed in your divine purpose. Following the revelation of good secrecy helps you live a quality life to the fullest. Divine purpose is rewarding.

If you can't hear, you can't detect the sound of a conclusion. Purpose has a sound, if you have ears, you will hear it. Purpose makes a call, if you listen, it will speak. If you refuse to listen to the conclusion of purpose, you will move around aimlessly. If you're aimless, life's results will also be aimless. Things don't just happen, they happen because someone or something made it happen. If you refuse to follow a divine call, you can't get a divine provision. Your destiny is tied to your breakthrough. Your wealth is in your divine purpose. If you derail from the track of destiny, you will impede your movement to abundance and heavenly rewards. To be the best on earth, you must follow real purpose. To be told 'Well-done' in heaven, you must follow real purpose. Real purpose is God's intention for you, not your intention for yourself. Real purpose is predestined. Predestination is divinely pre-planned before creation. No one plans better than God. If God says He has a plan for you, better drop yours, and consider yourself privileged. Embracing divine purpose is embracing God's plan. When He executes His plan, it's always a masterpiece. Why do your own thing when you can have something better?

To find real purpose, you must go back to the One who has the best definition of destiny in His divine book. The Bible teaches the Way, the Truth, and the Life. The way of purpose is the Bible. The truth of purpose is the Bible. The life of purpose is the Bible. If you have missed your way, go back to the roadmap of destination; the Bible. If you are confused, hold onto the letter that sets free; the Bible. If you face a death sentence from this world's unending problems, run to the source of living water; the Bible.

Real people find real purpose from the real book. Finding real purpose won't leave you guessing about the future. Real purpose is a conviction, addiction, and addition. When you stick to your calling, you stick to life. The devil may come raging, but keep braving. You are a lion, because you're the child of the Lion of the tribe of Judah. Lions don't get intimidated. They are bold. Remember, the righteous are as bold as a lion!

ABOUT THE AUTHOR

Kenneth Nkemnacho is a writer, teacher, mentor, inspirational speaker, and radio/television host. He has authored lots of books and articles which major on developing individuals for corporate excellence.

Kenneth is the CEO of Kenneth Vision Media; an organisation committed to writing, publishing, and content creations.

As a prolific blogger and social media expert, he founded www.successinks.com; a success and personal development blog that daily motivates and inspire people to beat the odds and excel in their chosen endeavours.

Kenneth is married to Ruth, and they are blessed with two children; Favour and Joshua.

If you would like him to feature as a speaker in your conferences, events, seminars, workshops, or training programmes, please send an email to Kenneth@kennethvisionmedia.com.

www.ingramcontent.com/pod-product-compliance
Lightning Source LLC
Chambersburg PA
CBHW060156070426
42447CB00033B/1502